metalcraft
for the home

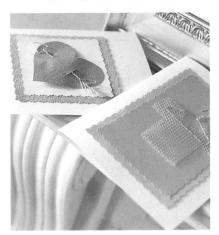

metalcraft

for the home

20 step-by-step craft projects

LISA BROWN

NORTH LIGHT BOOKS
CINCINNATI, OHIO

First published in the UK in 2001 by David & Charles
Brunel House, Newton Abbot, Devon
ISBN 0 7153 1144 1

First published in North America
in 2001 by North Light Books
an imprint of F&W Publications, Inc.
1507 Dana Avenue
Cincinnati, OH 45207
1-800/289-0963
ISBN 1-58180-228-5

A catalogue record for this book is available
from the British Library.

Commissioning editor LINDSAY PORTER
Art editor ALI MYER
Desk editor JENNIFER PROVERBS
Photography LUCINDA SYMONS
Step photography BRIAN HATTON

Printed in Italy by STIGE Turin
for David & Charles

Working with metal in these projects is straightforward and safe provided proper
precautions are taken. Protective gloves, goggles and clothing should be worn whenever
you are working with the harder metals and wires. In particular, protective gloves should
be worn when cutting and filing any of these materials.
The author and publisher has made every effort to ensure that all instructions in this book
are accurate and safe, and therefore cannot accept any responsibility for any injury
incurred in the making of these projects.

contents

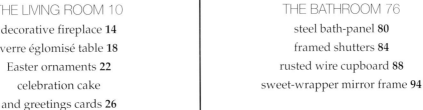

introduction

Part of my work as a journalist and author for interior design and craft publications has involved coming up with accessible ideas for making useful and beautiful items for the home. In my experience, projects using 'soft' materials such as fabric, paper and trimmings always spring to mind more readily than ideas for harder materials, where the tendency is to steer away from anything that might require too many specialist tools or which appears to be in any way dangerous to work with. For many, metal is one of the most intimidating materials in this category, and anything to do with it is usually avoided before even exploring the possibilities. However, over the years, I have come to realize just how accessible and interesting a material metal is.

I've discovered that there are many easy-to-work-with metals available that are far removed from the wrought iron we normally associate with this material. I've also found the creative potential of metal to be enormous. My first few successful projects then spurred me on to explore more ideas, the result of which is this book.

The discovery of metals marked a fundamental step in the progress of human civilization. Subsequently, our ability, with the help of specific tools such as rolling mills and drawplates, to manipulate metals into sheet and wire

Delicate wirework recalls the filigree work of the past.

form has enabled us to mould it into almost any shape imaginable. This, coupled with the fact that metal can then be cut, twisted, pierced and folded, makes it a most attractive and useful medium with which to work.

Reclaim metal objects for decorative use.

The use of metal sheet and wire goes back thousands of years, and these forms have always been used both for function and for decoration. These days, in the area of craft, metalwork is often associated with such arts as the tinware of Mexico or the wirework of Zimbabwe, both of which utilize cheap, recycled materials. In the West, we have the choice of buying metals from specialist suppliers at relatively low cost or recycling metals for purely decorative purposes.

Three forms of metal are used in this book: sheet metal, wire and wire mesh, the latter being a material that seems to combine the qualities of the first two.

Flat or sheet metal is used in an assortment of forms. The most widely known types are the embossing foils used in many crafts. Of the finer of these, I have explored the use of silver leaf, a metal so thin that it is almost impossible to feel when handled, and foil sweet wrappers, an interesting idea for recycling metal. Among the heavier embossing foils are thicker flat metals such as tin (another easily recycled metal), pewter and galvanized steel. Sheet aluminium is one

Thin sheet metal can be cut and embossed easily.

Chickenwire replaces a door panel, converting a junk cupboard into a stylish piece of furniture.

of the most satisfying flat metals to work with as it is easy to cut, lightweight and very malleable, and because of these qualities it has been used in a number of the designs in the book.

The majority of the wires used in this book are readily available, with the exception of a very thick aluminium wire which can be purchased from a specialist supplier by mail order (see Resources). The rest are manufactured for everyday household, gardening and craft use in an enormous range of thicknesses and metal types, providing an interesting choice of colours. As well as being used in its single

form, wire can also be adapted to enhance strength, flexibility and decoration by twisting it, a method that has been used in several of the designs.

Wire meshes start with crude chicken wire at one end of the spectrum and work through to the finer meshes, which are relatively new on the market and were developed initially as a sculpting aid. Their moulding and decorative qualities offer huge potential for craft possibilities.

The stronger sheet metals and very thick wires are available from specialist metal suppliers, while the finer foils,

Woven strips of sheet metal form a striking chair seat.

wires and meshes can be purchased from craft suppliers and hardware shops (see Resources). All the types of metal mentioned above are fully described in the Materials and Equipment section at the back of the book. One of the great things about working with metal is that the materials are relatively inexpensive and can be conveniently purchased in small quantities, even from the specialist suppliers. I have endeavoured to keep the designs throughout the book as accessible as possible, so the majority can be made up using a basic set of tools, with just a few requiring other inexpensive extras, such as tin snips and wire cutters. One project only, a galvanized steel bath-panel, will need to be cut by the metal suppliers in the same way as a timber merchant would cut timber. The rest of the projects can all be worked entirely at home.

Putting this book together has opened my eyes even further to the possibilities of this fascinating material, through designs

Wire mesh can be moulded with ease into decorative shapes.

and ideas in which metal in its many forms has been transformed into the most delicate and decorative object, or something strong, stylish and practical. I hope these designs will take away the fear of metal as something that is hard and uncompromising to work with, and will be an inspiration to explore the potential of this diverse and exciting material to the full.

Lisa Brown

the
living room

the living room

Living rooms are designed as areas in which to relax after a hard day's work or at the weekend, providing a haven from the ordinary clutter of everyday life. The designs for this area have been devised to reflect this function. In this room, I have branched away from the urban minimalist ideas so often associated with metal and come up with ideas in which the emphasis is on their visual impact and decorative qualities. The ideas in this chapter comprise two substantial ideas and two ornamental, decorative concepts – all of which, as well as being functional, are stunning to look at.

Existing fire surrounds can sometimes be a problem in a new home. A solution can be found, however, by covering the fire surround or replacing it with a simple boxed version, which works in both a traditional and a modern interior and provides a blank canvas awaiting decoration. This is an ideal surface on which to use metal foils, as they can be pinned into position and are hardwearing when fixed. The fire surround included here was inspired by several sources, though predominantly Mexican and folk-art designs, and uses motifs depicting suns, hearts and stars and a decorative scallop design. All are cut from lightweight aluminium and copper foils. The scallops and motifs have been further decorated using an embossing technique.

It is hard to think of metal in any form as being lighter than a feather, but silver and gold leaf are the finest sheet metal forms available. This interesting medium was used to great effect in a method called verre églomisé, or 'leafing on to glass'. This technique is more usually used on small objects, but here it was used on a large glass tabletop. The technique looks best on a

Fine mesh adds an unexpected and eyecatching dimension to greetings cards for any occasion.

tabletop that can be fitted into a recessed area. The glass is painted on the underside with a specialist adhesive mixture and the silver leaf is laid carefully on top. The result resembles an antique mirror, the silver leaf tending to break up slightly in places to give a distressed effect. This style works particularly well with old wrought-iron tables, so start scouring your local junk shops for similar furniture.

The reflective qualities of this tabletop bring light into a darker area of the living room.

Whatever is put behind metal mesh becomes diffused and in some ways more attractive, in rather the same way that old-fashioned hats with net make older women look younger! This thought inspired a project involving some gorgeous decorative eggs made from fine moulded mesh and organza ribbon. A decorative item has been placed inside each one – a combination of eggs, flowers and feathers. Individually, these eggs make an ideal gift, particularly at Easter, and would also grace any mantelpiece or shelf all year round. Grouped together, they can be hung from a small twig tree to be used as a table centrepiece or party decoration. This idea can easily be translated to suit other festivities; for example, at Christmas the eggs can be turned into round baubles, enclosing tin stars or sweets to hang on the tree.

On the same note of celebration, the final project for this room is a decorative birthday cake, made from wire mesh and jewellery wire, and finished with a decorative ribbon and real birthday cake candles. This is designed to make a memorable gift for a loved one – a lot more substantial and longer lasting than the real thing! Using similar materials to the cake, but in a finer mesh, cards were made for special occasions. The fine mesh can be cut easily into motifs: here, a baby T-shirt for a new-baby card, a pretty bouquet for Mother's Day and an arrow-pierced heart for a Valentine.

decorative fireplace

Add interest to a plain, yet

brightly coloured, fireplace with

embossed Mexican-style motifs

reproduced in aluminium and

copper foils.

A plain boxed fireplace makes an unusual alternative to the more traditional variety, and is also a great way of temporarily covering up an unwanted existing fireplace. This simple shape lends itself to decoration, here with a striking Mexican-inspired design. Mexico and other South American countries are a huge source of inspiration for designs using metal foils and recycled tin, and here traditional motifs in a combination of aluminium and copper foils have been placed on a fuchsia-pink background.

materials & equipment

tracing paper

pencil

scissors

masking tape

42 gauge (0.1mm)
copper and
aluminium foils

newspaper

ballpoint pen

pinking shears

panel pins

hammer

STEP 1

Trace the sun, star and heart motifs from the templates on pages 140–141. Trim the pattern shapes, then tape the sun and heart to squares of copper foil, and the star to aluminium foil. Using a pencil, lightly redraw over the lines to transfer the images to the foil. Repeat to transfer as many motifs as necessary for your fireplace.

STEP 2

Remove the pattern shapes and place the pieces of foil face down on a cushion of newspaper. Using a ballpoint pen, draw firmly over the main lines to emboss the designs into the metal. Add the detail with dots and short lines.

STEP 3

Working on the front of the foil, cut out the stars and suns with scissors, cutting just outside the embossed outline. Cut out the hearts with pinking shears to give them a zigzag edge.

STEP 4

Cut two bands of aluminium foil, each 5cm (2in) deep and long enough to fit across the width of the fireplace. If your fireplace is very wide, cut four half-widths of foil and butt them together later when you fix them to the fireplace. Use the template of the wide scalloped band on page 140 to cut out the scalloped bands, then place them on newspaper.

Emboss patterns into the back of the foil using dots, lines and stars, following the template. Cut bands of foil 2.5cm (1in) deep to fit the fireplace supports, then use the template of the narrow scalloped band on page 141 to cut out the scalloped band. Emboss as before, following the template.

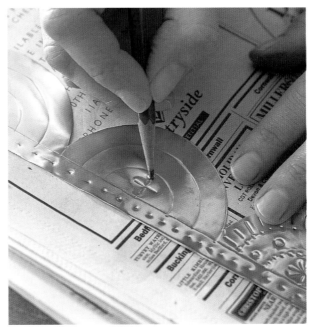

STEP 5

Using masking tape, fix the scalloped bands, embossed side up, in position on the fireplace. Tape the suns, hearts and stars in place between the bands. When you are satisfied that all the motifs are evenly spaced, fix the decorations to the fireplace using short panel pins and a hammer.

verre églomisé table

Silver leaf is an often overlooked

form of metal and can be used to

great effect on the underside

of glass to create a convincing

antique-mirrored look.

The process of silver-leafing glass is called verre églomisé, and lends itself particularly to the decoration of tabletops where the underside is rarely touched. The method involves making up a clear adhesive using gelatine, methylated spirit and distilled water. This is painted on to the glass and then silver leaf is applied directly on top. The result is a soft, antique-mirrored effect with a slightly distressed look, enhanced by the tiny cracks in the silver leaf. The tabletop is placed in the recess of a complementary painted wrought-iron table.

materials & equipment

4mm (⅛in) glass, cut to size of table recess

methylated spirit (turpentine)

kitchen roll

saucepan

heatproof glass bowl

stirring implement

distilled water

2 gelatine capsules

wide and narrow paintbrushes

silver leaf

gilder's tip

petroleum jelly

scalpel

cotton wool

shellac

STEP 1
Clean the piece of glass thoroughly with methylated spirit on a couple of pieces of kitchen roll to remove dust, dirt and grease.

STEP 2
Using a saucepan and heatproof glass bowl as a bain-marie, dissolve two gelatine capsules in the bowl containing 180ml (6fl oz) distilled water and 60ml (2fl oz) methylated spirit (turpentine).

STEP 3
Starting from a corner of the glass, use a wide paintbrush to paint the still warm adhesive over a section approximately the size of six pieces of silver leaf. Apply the silver leaf immediately, as described in steps 4–6.

STEP 4
Silver leaf is extremely fine and can stick if picked up with fingers, so it is advisable to use a gilder's tip to pick up the leaf. Add a touch of petroleum jelly to the gilder's tip to help it pick up more efficiently.

STEP 5
Lift the leaf with the tip and hover it in position over the glued corner section of the glass, allowing the adhesive to pull it down. Apply the next piece of leaf, slightly overlapping the edge of the first piece, then continue until the glued section is covered. Do not touch the leaf with your fingers; it will look creased at this stage, but will flatten when dry.

STEP 6
Fill any large gaps that occur with sections of leaf cut with a scalpel. Cut on the used side of the leaf book so you are not cutting though other layers of unused leaf. Continue gluing and adding full sections of silver leaf to cover one side of the glass completely. Leave to dry for 24 hours.

STEP 7
Gently rub the loose pieces of leaf from the table with a piece of cotton wool.

STEP 8
Using the narrower paintbrush, apply shellac for protection to help prevent the silver from tarnishing. When dry, lay the glass, silvered side down, on the table.

Easter ornaments

Silvery mesh eggs enclose pretty,

lightweight objects for gifts,

decoration and display.

These delicate objects make an ideal Easter gift – present them individually filled with a feather, blown quail's egg or a silk flower. For decoration, make some to hang from an Easter 'tree' of twisted willow branches sprayed silver. Alternatively, display one on your own mantelpiece or shelf, or suspend it near a window for an eyecatching effect. Each egg is simply constructed from silvery wire mesh, moulded in two halves around an egg shape. These are then joined together, holding a decorative filler of your choice, and finished off with a ribbon.

materials & equipment

eggs for moulds
(use ornamental
plaster or marble
eggs, or hardboiled
hen and duck eggs)

pencil

paper

scissors

wire modelling mesh,
5mm (¼in) diamond
pattern

permanent marker pen

protective gloves

heavy-duty scissors

decorative objects, such
as silk flowers, feathers
and blown quail's eggs

superglue

organza ribbon

fine ribbon or
sewing thread

SAFETY NOTE

Although the mesh is
fine, it is advisable
to wear protective
gloves when handling
cut edges.

STEP 1
Draw an oval shape
on paper, to measure
a little larger than the
egg you are using
as a mould.

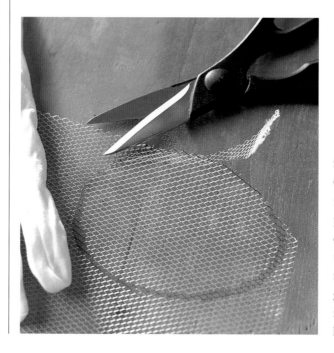

STEP 2
Cut out the egg-shaped
template and use a
permanent marker pen to
draw around the paper
template on to the wire
mesh. Wearing protective
gloves, cut out the shape
from the mesh using
heavy-duty scissors.

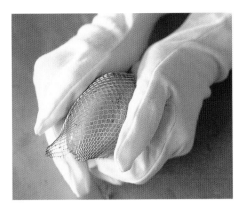

STEP 3
Wearing protective gloves, press, stretch and smooth the wire mesh around the egg, trying not to make tucks at the sides. Slip the mesh off the egg. Make a second shape in the same way.

STEP 4
Still wearing protective gloves, use heavy-duty scissors to trim the irregular edges, to give a neat shape that is slightly larger than half the mould egg.

STEP 5
Overlapping the cut edges and enclosing a decoration, gently press the two mesh halves together. The edges will catch together in places, but secure the join with tiny drops of superglue.

STEP 6
Tie organza ribbon over the join and knot it at the top. Tie a bow and trim the ends with either a diagonal or a V-shaped cut. Use as an ornament, Easter gift or hanging decoration, suspending it with sewing thread or fine ribbon.

celebration cake and greetings cards

Make your own cake to last and

cards to remember using a

combination of silver mesh and

jewellery wire.

A handmade cake always means more to the receiver than one that is bought, but if your cakes are always falling flat here is a foolproof way of providing something with plenty of rise that will last and is guaranteed to delight. It is simply constructed from one of the stronger versions of the wire mesh often used for sculpting. Decoration is added with a fine wire coil at the top of each tier and a pretty bow to trim the base, while real birthday candles soften the effect.

materials & equipment

pencil

paper

pair of compasses/
round objects

scissors

permanent marker pen

wire modelling mesh,
6.8mm (¼in) diamond
pattern

protective gloves

heavy-duty scissors

wire cutters

modelling wire

10 amp fuse wire

tweezers

superglue

0.6mm silver-plated
jewellery wire for coils
(see page 128
for method)

ribbon

birthday cake candles

SAFETY NOTE

Although the mesh is
fine, it is advisable
to wear protective
gloves when handling
cut edges.

STEP 1

Using a pair of compasses or suitable round objects, draw out on paper two circles for the tiers of the cake, the first with a radius of 3.5cm (1⅜in), the second with a radius of 4.5cm (1¾in). Cut out each circle.

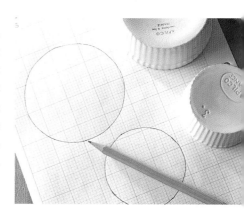

STEP 2

Using a permanent marker pen, draw around the two paper circles on to the wire mesh, making each circle slightly larger than its template. Wearing protective gloves, cut out the circles using heavy-duty scissors. Cut a side piece for each tier, each one measuring the length of the circumference of the matching wire mesh circle. Using wire cutters, cut three lengths of modelling wire each measuring the length of the longer side piece, and two lengths each measuring the length of the shorter side piece.

STEP 3

Join the wires into rings the same size as the paper templates. Overlap the ends and bind them with fuse wire. Take a mesh side piece and turn in a small fold along one long edge and then, overlapping the ends, wrap the folded edge around a corresponding wire ring. Do the same with the second side piece and wire ring.

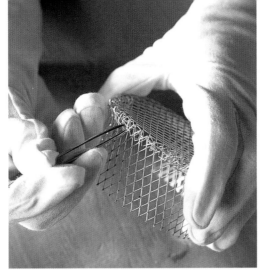

STEP 4

Fit a wire mesh circle over the top of each ring and turn in the edges. Use tweezers to pinch together any pairs of wires along the edge and push them to the inside.

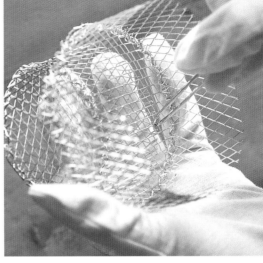

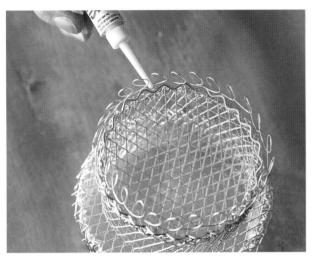

STEP 5

Fit the smaller tier on top of the larger one. Some of the wire mesh along the raw edge of the top tier will cling to the top of the lower tier. Use the tweezers to turn in all the wires neatly.

STEP 6

Superglue the additional rings of modelling wire around the top of each tier. Make two coils of silver-plated jewellery wire the same length as the circumference of the circles. Stretch and flatten the coils, and make into two rings; bind the joins with fuse wire. Glue a ring around the top of each tier. Add the final ring of modelling wire to the base by bending and turning in the lower edge.

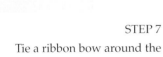

SAFETY NOTE

Do not leave lighted candles unattended.

STEP 7

Tie a ribbon bow around the base of the cake. Taper the ends of the birthday cake candles and twist them gently into the mesh of the top tier. Place the cake on a plate before lighting the candles.

Y̶ou can also make cards for different occasions using a combination of the finer silver mesh and jewellery wire. Suggestions are provide here for Valentine's day, Mother's Day and the birth of a new baby.

STEP 1

Cut out squares and rectangles of coloured paper or lightweight card using paper edging scissors, to be used as the background for the motifs. Fold a piece of paper, then draw and cut out half a heart shape against the fold. Open this out and use it as a template to cut out the pink heart. Use the same method to cut out a T-shirt shape from plain paper.

STEP 2

Using heavy-duty scissors, cut a square of wire mesh to act as wrapping for the bouquet design. Fold two opposite corners to the centre and scrunch up the base. Tie it with a bow of wire-edged ribbon, cutting the ends of the bow into a V shape.

STEP 3

Fold a small piece of wire mesh, place the top of the T-shirt template on the fold line and cut around it. Again cutting through both layers of wire mesh, cut out a neck shape on the folded edge.

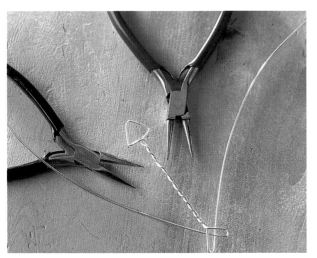

STEP 4

Make an arrow from the silver-plated jewellery wire. Using round-nosed pliers, bend the wire in half and then make a bend at each side to form the arrowhead. Holding both ends of the wire with the flat-nosed pliers and with the arrowhead in your other hand, twist the two ends to make the shaft. Use the round-nosed pliers to bend each end out and then back on itself to make the first pair of feathers.

STEP 5

Twist the ends together for a couple of turns, as before. Repeat this process to the end of the arrow and trim the ends if necessary. Use the same bending and twisting techniques to make the coat hanger. To do this, first bend the triangle, then twist the ends together. Snip off one end close to the twist. Bend the other end to make the curve of the hook and then trim.

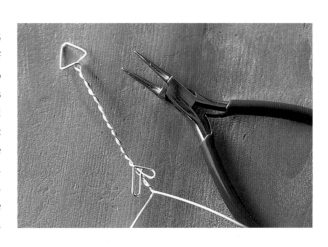

STEP 6

Assemble the cards. Use paper adhesive to fix the coloured squares and rectangles in place. Use strong all-purpose adhesive to attach the bouquet wrapper and then the ribbon roses. Slip the hanger inside the mesh T-shirt and use a few small dabs of adhesive to attach these to the card. Using a craft knife, cut slits in the heart large enough to take the arrow. Insert this and glue the heart in place. Fold the cards to complete.

the
kitchen

the kitchen

Retro style is the new look for fashionable interiors, particularly in the kitchen, where 1950s décor combined with hearty home cooking is making a big comeback. Old-style American refrigerators with a steel finish or soft pastel colours of pale green, blue and yellow are now more popular than the common white version. In the same vein, utilitarian metal finishes are replacing the façades of other conventional appliances such as ovens and washing machines or kitchen worktops.

Metal finishes have always been popular in the professional kitchen, where practicality is of the utmost importance. The simple and graphic style of these pieces is now directly influencing our domestic interiors, with the seamless moulded shapes of free-standing units much in demand. Perhaps the best way to achieve this look is with a combination of old, new and handmade items. The shelves, table, chair and splashback in this chapter provide a great start as far as handmade pieces go, and are also simple enough in themselves to combine beautifully with any existing kitchen. The first three items use aluminium, available from specialist metal suppliers in sheet form, in a variety of widths and thicknesses. It is easy to work with, being fairly malleable and simple to cut. The splashback combines a variety of metal foils and is decorated with

Soften the urban look of aluminium with complementary pastel colours.

panels cut from decorative tin cans. The foils are available from craft suppliers and the tin cans are sourced from supermarkets and delicatessens.

Old tables with enamel or zinc tops are currently very fashionable, with prices now reflecting their popularity. Fortunately, it is simple to recreate this retro style at a fraction of the price, using a junk table neatly covered with sheet aluminium. It can be used as a stylish breakfast table in a small kitchen or as an extra work surface to slot alongside fitted units. Newly made, it looks pristine, but it will inevitably become scratched and slightly dented, which will only add to its charm.

Combine the table with a pretty chair with a woven seat made from the same sheet aluminium. This chair looks stunning on its own, painted in a colour complementary to your kitchen, or would work beautifully in a group where each chair is painted in a slightly different pastel shade. This method of weaving aluminium would also work well on a square or rectangular footstool or barstool.

Shelves without brackets are sleek and minimal and provide an ideal area for showing off kitchenware, from the very decorative to the purely practical. They are simplest when made completely straight, but for extra interest a right-angled piece can be placed at one

Aluminium sheeting was used to cover the table and create a decorative front for the drawer.

end. This style of shelf is best fixed into a corner or alcove. Wrapped in sheet aluminium and embellished with chrome stud fixings, the shelves' reflective qualities draw the eye to any display.

Tin foils and tin cans can be surprisingly decorative and are recycled to great effect in many countries. The splashback was inspired by the wonderful Mexican use of shaped and patterned foil, often seen on frames and mirrors, combined with decorative tin cans produced mostly in Europe. The cans to look for are those with a design printed directly on to the tin. The idea works well as a splashback, but could be modified to make a decorative panel or mirror frame.

These projects require none of the specialist tools that you would normally associate with metalwork, such as soldering irons, and can all be made at home with the standard tools used for basic DIY projects. The shelves require a small amount of woodworking, and the tabletop and splashback both use pre-cut MDF (medium-density fiberboard).

aluminium tabletop

This small kitchen table with its

satin metal surface combines the

practicality of the professional

worktop with the homely feel of

the post-war kitchen.

This table originally had an ugly red formica top and dark wood legs, but has been turned into a retro-style table which sits comfortably in either a sleek contemporary kitchen or a funky, colourful environment. Sheet aluminium forms a new surface, and the legs were given a simple paint effect. This style is inspired by the zinc and enamel tabletops popular in the 1950s, now classed as antiques with accordingly high price tags. Yet small kitchen tables are one of the cheapest junk shop items, so this look can be recreated easily, at relatively low cost.

preparation

Remove the original tabletop and replace it with a piece of 15mm (½in) thick MDF cut to size. Rub down the old paint or varnish on the legs with sandpaper to achieve a good 'key', ready for painting. Apply two or more coats of cream oil-based paint, allowing each coat to dry. Use a dry brush to drag a little pale blue oil-based paint over the surface to create a distressed look.

Cut the aluminium sheet 4.5cm (1¾in) larger all round than the measurement of the new MDF tabletop. To do this, score along the cutting line firmly with a craft knife and ruler, then carefully flex the metal so that it breaks cleanly. Wearing protective gloves, rub a sanding block along all the cut edges to make them safe.

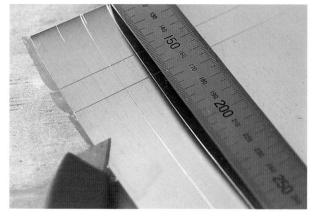

STEP 1
Using a craft knife and metal ruler, score lines lightly on the underside of the aluminium sheet, 3cm (1¼in) in from the edges and again 1.5cm (½in) in from the first line. This makes it easier to bend the metal to fit around the edge of the tabletop.

STEP 2
Using the tin snips and wearing the protective gloves, cut each corner of the metal sheet as shown.

STEP 3

Place the new MDF tabletop on to the metal sheet and gently bend the two longer sides along the score lines, tucking the small tab around the corners at each end.

STEP 4

Use a bradawl to pierce small holes in the metal about 6cm (2½in) apart, as pilot holes for the panel pins. Then hammer in pins to secure the metal to the MDF.

STEP 5

Bend the shorter end pieces along the score lines and fix in place with the panel pins as before. Fix the tabletop to the legs using right-angled brackets and screws.

STEP 6

This step is optional, depending on whether or not your table has a drawer. First remove the drawer handle. Cut a panel from the sheet aluminium to fit the drawer front, rounding off the corners for a neat finish. Position the panel on the drawer front, pierce small holes at each corner with a bradawl and fix in place using small round-headed screws. Replace the drawer handle.

woven chair-seat

An ordinary kitchen chair is

transformed with a stylish woven

metal seat and complementary

pastel paint.

Old square kitchen chairs can be picked up for a song from junk shops, particularly when the seat is broken, as is often the case. A practical and stylish way to solve this problem is by making a new seat from woven aluminium strips, cut from sheet aluminium and filed down so as to avoid any nasty scratches. They are then cut to fit the dimensions of the chair, and woven in the traditional way. The result is attractive and contemporary, and works well if the rest of the chair is given a lick of paint in one of the stylish pastel colours now available.

materials & equipment

junk chair

sandpaper

oil-based paint

paintbrush

24 gauge (0.5mm) sheet aluminium, for chair seat

permanent marker pen

metal ruler

craft knife

protective gloves

sanding pad suitable for metal

tin snips

panel pins

hammer

preparation

Sand the chair ready for painting, then apply two coats of oil-based paint in a colour of your choice, allowing each coat to dry before applying the next.

Remove and discard the old chair seat, leaving a frame on which to weave the aluminium strips.

STEP 1

Lay the aluminium sheet flat and use a ruler and permanent pen to mark it into strips approximately 4cm (10in) wide, or a width close to this that will divide evenly into the width and depth measurements of the seat. The strips will each need to be about 25cm (9¾in) longer than the width and depth measurements. The chair shown required nine strips for the depth and seven strips for the width. Using a metal ruler and craft knife, score the aluminium sheet along the marked lines, making two or three firm strokes.

STEP 2

Wearing protective gloves, take the sheet and carefully flex one strip at a time along its length until it breaks cleanly.

STEP 3
Using a sanding pad suitable for metal, smooth off both edges of all the strips to blunt them.

STEP 4
Mark the central point on the back of the chair seat frame, then place one metal strip centrally on top of the mark, bending the ends loosely around the back and front of the frame to secure. Add all but the final two end strips in this way, working outwards to each side.

STEP 5
Because the chair is narrower along the back frame, you will need to cut a rectangular section from the two end strips, using tin snips, to allow them to fit around the upright posts. Keep this strip to its original width at the front.

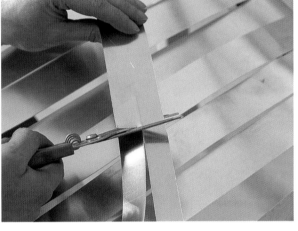
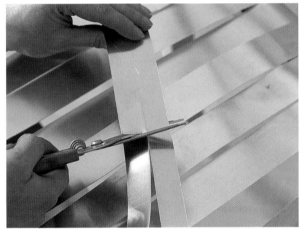

STEP 6
Hammer in a panel pin to keep these last two strips in place at each side.

STEP 7
Begin to weave the horizontal strips in a simple, plain weave pattern (over one, under one). Continue until the seat is complete, then bend the ends around the chair frame in the same way as before to secure.

STEP 8
Turn the chair upside down, then snip off the excess metal at the end of each strip using tin snips. Secure each strip to the chair frame by hammering in two or three panel pins.

aluminium shelves

Aluminium shelves without brackets for support are practical as well as decorative and bring a stylish, minimalist look to a contemporary kitchen.

A shelf without brackets has a simple, uncluttered profile that lends itself to the clean lines of a modern kitchen. This is enhanced by covering it with aluminium sheeting, a reflective surface that looks as good as it is practical. The shelf bases are made from readily available radiator shelves which have been customized and covered to achieve the required effect. The instructions are for a long, straight shelf that sits elegantly on the middle of the wall, and a shorter shelf with a right-angled corner that fits into a recessed area.

materials & equipment

radiator shelves, or lengths of wood, (measuring 13cm (5⅛in) deep after shaped edges are removed) with invisible fittings, small and large

jigsaw

lengths of 12 x 45mm (½ x 1¾in) timber

wood saw

wood adhesive

panel pins

hammer

sheet hardboard

craft knife

metal ruler

24 gauge (0.5mm) sheet aluminium, to cover shelves

protective gloves

tin snips

wet-and-dry paper and sanding block

bradawl

mirror screws with decorative chrome screw covers

screwdriver

STEP 1

Using a jigsaw, cut off the shaped edges from the radiator shelves.

STEP 2

For the straight shelf, cut two strips of timber to fit across the short ends of the shelf, then cut another to fit along the front edge, overlapping the timber on the short ends. For the right-angled shelf, leave a 4.5cm (1¾in) gap at the left-hand end as shown. Glue and pin the timber in place, then allow the adhesive to dry.

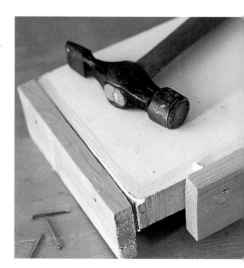

STEP 3

Cut timber to form the frame for the right-angled section. Cut one upright piece 20cm (8in) long, another 15.5cm (6⅛in) long, and one top piece 14.5cm (5¾in) long. Glue and pin the pieces to form the right-angled frame as shown.

STEP 4
Using a craft knife and metal ruler, cut hardboard rectangles to fit on the undersides of the shelves and on both sides of the right-angled frame. Pin in place.

straight shelf

For the straight shelf, cut out the aluminium sheet using template (A), again extending where indicated to fit your shelf, but in this instance place the tab section at both ends (there is no need for a mitre) to wrap around the shelf. Repeat steps 8 and 9 to finish. Fix the straight and angled shelves on to the wall using the invisible fittings supplied with the radiator shelves.

STEP 5
For the angled shelf, enlarge the templates for the straight shelf (A) and right-angled frame (B) on pages 134–135, and extend for the straight shelf where indicated on template (A) to fit. Wearing protective gloves, cut the aluminium sheet to size from the two templates using a craft knife and metal ruler. To cut straight edges, score three times firmly, then flex to make a clean break. To score, just draw the knife lightly along the ruler once. Still wearing protective gloves, use tin snips to cut the smaller corners. Sand the raw edges with a sanding block for a smooth finish. Use a spare piece of wood as a straight edge to bend the metal to shape.

STEP 6
Wearing protective gloves, wrap the metal cut from template (B) around the right-angled piece, making sure that all the corners are tucked in neatly. Pin securely in place.

STEP 7
Position the main shelf piece carefully so that there are no gaps at the mitred point.

STEP 8
Pin all the edges securely in place.

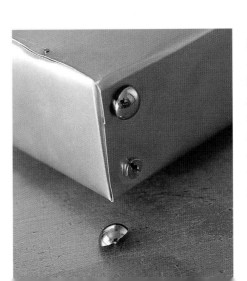

STEP 9
At each corner and at intervals along the length, make a hole with a bradawl, insert a mirror screw, then screw on a decorative chrome screw cover. Fix to the wall using the invisible fittings supplied.

tin splashback

Colourful cans flattened and framed with scalloped foil make charming decorations on a simple tin splashback.

Tiles are the obvious choice for a sink splashback and increasingly, in modern kitchens, stainless steel panels are used, although they are prone to water staining. As a special surface is needed in this area, choose something a little different. This splashback is made from a foil-covered sheet of MDF, decorated with 'pictures' cut from decorative tin cans. Each picture is framed with a contrasting brass foil edge. The overall look is Mediterranean, due mainly to the strong cobalt-blue units, enhanced by the tin can panels depicting exotic contents.

materials & equipment

piece of 12mm (½in) exterior grade MDF (medium-density fiberboard), to fit above sink

yacht varnish (spar varnish)

paintbrush

length of 42 gauge (0.1mm) aluminium foil, to cover MDF

pencil

scissors

short panel pins

hammer

printed tin cans, clean and dry with lids removed

tin opener

protective gloves

tin shears

hide mallet

ruler

36 gauge (0.1mm) brass foil, for trim

small coin

ballpoint pen (optional)

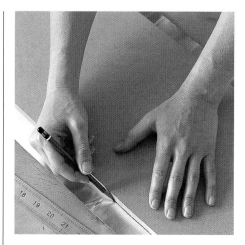

STEP 1
Seal the MDF (medium-density fiberboard) panel with two coats of yacht varnish (spar varnish). Place the panel on the aluminium foil. Mark the position of the MDF, allowing enough room to overlap the edges. Trim the foil to size with scissors.

STEP 2
Replace the panel on the foil and fold the metal over the edges. Snip a square of foil from each corner so that you can fold it neatly. Attach the foil to the MDF using a hammer and short panel pins.

STEP 3
Remove the bases from the tin cans using a tin opener. Wearing protective gloves, use tin shears to cut open the cans along the side seam.

STEP 4

Neatly cut away the rolled lip at
the top and bottom of the cans.
Trim off any small spurs of metal
and dispose of them carefully.

STEP 5

Place the cans on a flat surface
and hammer the metal flat
using a hide mallet.

STEP 6

Decide on the size you
want your picture squares
to be, then measure and
trim down the metal cans,
making sure you remove
any sharp spurs as you cut.

STEP 7

Place the metal squares at equal distances along the splashback, allowing enough room around each for the brass trim. Attach the squares to the splashback along their edges with panel pins.

STEP 8

To make the trim, cut strips of brass foil 2cm (¾in) wide. Draw a line 3mm (⅛in) in from the top edge of each strip. Draw around half of a small coin on to the foil, to make a scalloped edge.

STEP 9

Cut out the scalloped trims using scissors. If desired, draw a simple pattern on to the back of the foil with a ballpoint pen to emboss the metal; otherwise, leave plain.

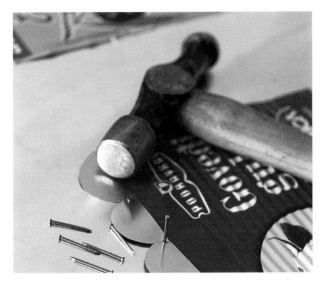

STEP 10

Place the trims around the tin squares, covering the cut edges of the metal. Attach the trims to the splashback with panel pins hammered in at the base of each scallop join and at the top centre of each scallop.

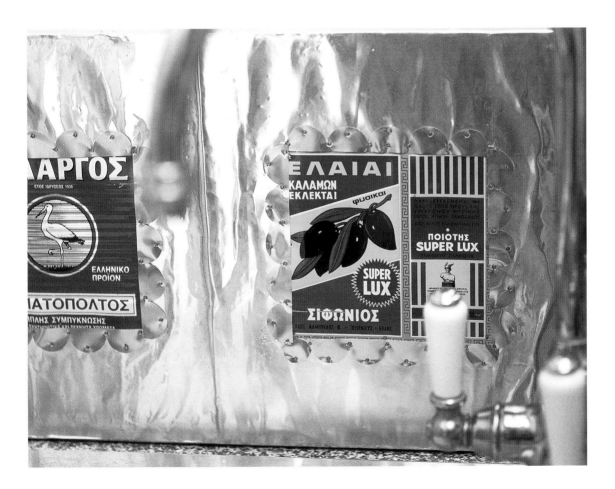

Scour delicatessens for brightly coloured decorative tins – olive and tomato tins from Greece and Spain often have the prettiest designs.

the
bedroom

the bedroom

Metal and wire seem hard materials to consider for use in a bedroom, but can be introduced into this area when thinking about the most important elements of the room. Apart from the bed, these are the curtains, wardrobes and lighting. As for the living room, for the bedroom I concentrated on decorative items and avoided anything too plain and architectural. With the exception of the cupboard, which is in a fashionable but traditional style, the other three designs are very decorative and quite sculptural in design. Getting the lighting right is of utmost importance in a bedroom and consequently two of the ideas tackle that problem, but in very different ways.

The first lighting design is very sculptural and sits equally well in a modern or traditional interior. It is composed of a single length of thick but incredibly lightweight and pliable aluminium wire that is bent and twisted to form a large, hollow sphere. This is then intertwined with plain white Christmas lights. It looks quite difficult to make as the design is so random, but the method behind forming the sphere is very logical and the aluminium wire is satisfying to work with, being so malleable. The sphere can be placed on the floor beside a low-level bed or on a table, from where it will cast pretty pinpricks of light around the whole room. It is a work of art in itself and is decorative whether lit or unlit.

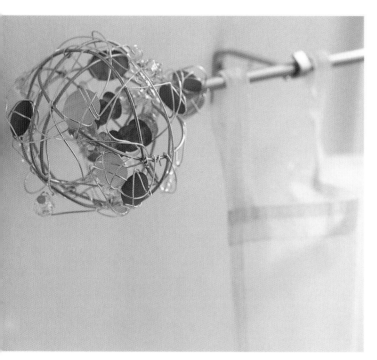

Plain curtain poles are embellished with beaded wire finials. The random tangle of wire creates a light, airy effect that is the perfect complement to sheer curtains.

The other lighting idea is in an altogether different style and was inspired by a combination of antique French crystal and beaded chandeliers and the more modern craft versions that are becoming popular. This light is designed for a pendant fitting and is made from a basic structure of two standard lamp rings, one larger than the other.

Between these sit decorative wire supports, incorporating a spiral design. These are threaded with a combination of glass beads in shades of mauve, pink and white. A clever detail is then added in the form of shaped glass discs which hang strategically all around the chandelier. As well as being decorative, these discs are designed to shield the eyes from the glare of the bulb.

The basic structure of this chandelier is surprisingly simple to create – its apparent complexity lies in the number and pattern of beads and embellishments.

Chicken wire is an understated material with great decorative potential. However, it is a tough material to work with, generally requiring the use of protective leather gloves and clothing and the right tools, so I have not explored here the more elaborate sculpting ideas to which it lends itself. However, I did want to introduce the material in a simple way and in the wardrobe project have shown how decorative it can be if used instead of a solid panel. We took an inexpensive 1940s wardrobe, picked up in a junk shop, and transformed it with white paint, chicken wire and some pretty checked fabric. All these elements transform the cupboard into a Swedish country-style wardrobe that now looks worth a lot more than it originally cost. The idea also works well if you remove the panels from standard kitchen units and replace them with chicken wire and then paint or spray the doors and wire white.

Finally, for the curtains, the unusual curtain pole finials and holdbacks were inspired by an astral theme. They are made from two strengths of galvanized wire threaded with light-catching beads in white and turquoise. The wire is wrapped to form a tangled mass with beads both inside and outside. The shades and tones of silver, white and turquoise work particularly well with light-coloured, floaty voile curtains.

Christmas-light sphere

This magical wire sphere threaded

with Christmas lights casts an

ambient glow that is ideal

for bedrooms.

W ire sculpted into interesting shapes is infiltrating the top end of the lighting market. Christmas lights are also becoming popular, with an array of styles and colours available. This unusual sphere encompasses both these elements in a lightweight sculpture that looks good whether lit or unlit. It is made from thick aluminium wire, which is surprisingly easy to work with. The wire is worked from one continuous length to aid strength, but if you run out more lengths can be added.

STEP 1
Using the wire from the roll, begin to crinkle it with your hands in a wiggly fashion, continuing until you have enough to form a circle with a diameter of about 40cm (16in).

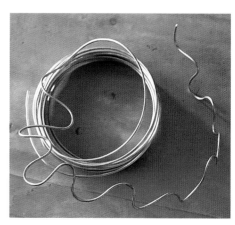

STEP 2
Join the circle by twisting the beginning of the wire around at this point and then continue to make a similar circle at right angles to the first.

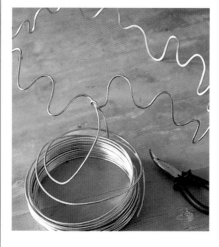

STEP 3
Bring the wire around again and twist to secure around the original circle, tightening with bent-nosed pliers if necessary, then again begin a new crinkly circle.

STEP 4

When the third circle is complete and secured in the same way as before, alter direction and make your new circles horizontally, this time twisting the wire each time it crosses another. You will need to wind your roll of wire into a tighter roll so that it passes more easily through gaps in the 'weave'.

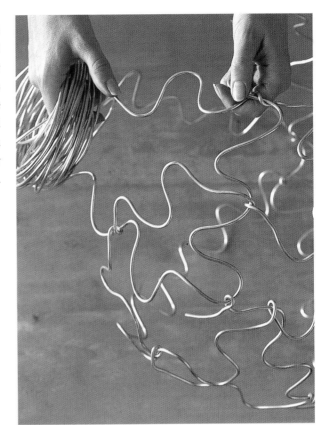

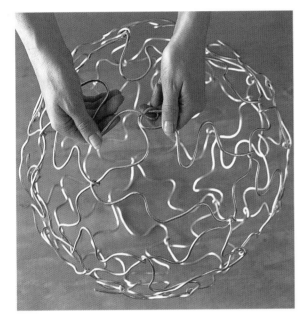

STEP 5

Continue in this manner until the sphere resembles an orderly tangle. You can easily adjust the form at this stage, pushing and pulling it into a spherical shape.

STEP 6

Mask each Christmas-light bulb with masking tape. Making sure the bulbs are not plugged in, spray the flex silver, then leave to dry. Remove the masking tape. Push and thread the Christmas lights through the sphere, wrapping them around the wire so that they are evenly spaced. This is quite time consuming, as you need to take the full Christmas light length in and out of the ball; wrap it into as small a roll as possible to enable you to do this more easily.

panelled wardrobe

The honeycombed effect of chicken wire brings a decorative element and a Swedish country-look to an old wardrobe.

Chicken wire is traditionally used for outdoor fencing, but over the years it has also been brought into the home. It has most commonly appeared in kitchens, used to adapt a cupboard into an airy and scavenger-free larder. Latterly, chicken wire has been used once again in a practical as well as decorative way for lining cupboard doors, this time for the storage of linen and glassware. Fabric is often placed behind the chicken wire, adding an extra dimension of colour and texture.

STEP 1
Sand all the woodwork ready for painting, then apply two coats of white oil-based paint, allowing each coat to dry before applying the next. Unscrew each door from its hinges and lay it face down. Carefully prize off the hardboard panels and remove the mirrors (if any, as in the cupboard shown here). If your doors have solid panels, cut these out using a jigsaw. Wipe away any dirt or dust that may have gathered in the recess.

STEP 2
Wearing protective gloves and goggles, and using wire cutters, cut a chicken wire panel for each door, making it slightly larger than the door panel. Cut as close to the honeycomb shape as possible to avoid leaving any sharp wire ends.

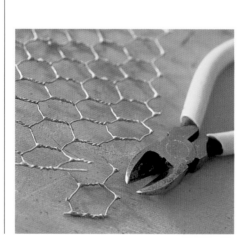

STEP 3
Still wearing protective gloves, snip out a small square from each corner of the chicken wire panel, so that it can be fitted neatly inside the recess.

STEP 4

Press the chicken wire gently into the recess, moulding the edges with your hands. Use a staple gun to secure the edges of the wire in place.

STEP 5

Cut a fabric panel for each door, 12cm (5in) longer than the panel and twice the width. Stitch a narrow double hem down each side and a casing 2cm (¾in) deep across the top and bottom edges.

STEP 6

Cut four lengths of expanding curtain wire, each about 2cm (¾in) wider than the panel. Screw a small eye into the end of each wire. Thread the wires though the casings of each fabric panel, gathering up the fabric slightly as you go.

This idea translates well for a kitchen cupboard. Dispense with the fabric and spray the chicken wire white for an easy-to-clean and attractive door front.

STEP 7

Screw the small hooks into the back of the door on either side of the chicken wire panels at top and bottom, then attach the fabric panels so that they hang quite taut.

wire chandelier

Curled wire and glittering beads

make an irresistible combination,

shown off to great decorative

effect in this modern update of a

luxurious French-style chandelier.

T raditional metal lamp rings are used to make up the top and bottom of the chandelier, anchoring the design together. Between these sit strong wire shapes threaded with pretty beads and embellished with curls. The beads have been chosen for their complementary shades and eyecatching combination of styles including matt, foiled and faceted. A scalloped wire fringe, threaded with beads, is fixed around the bottom ring. For extra decoration, and to shield the eyes from the glare of the bulb, glass discs are frosted and hung between the wire shapes.

materials & equipment

12 pre-drilled
glass shapes

etching spray

newspaper

20cm (8in) and
12cm (5in) diameter
metal lamp rings

silver metallic spray paint

2mm and 1.5mm
galvanized wire

0.6mm silver-plated
jewellery wire

pliers

assorted glass beads

round-nosed pliers

24 small earring hooks

small jewellery pliers

6 small split rings

SAFETY NOTE
Wire can be sharp, so
always wear goggles
to protect your eyes.

STEP 1

Apply etching spray to both sides of the glass shapes. In a well-ventilated area, lay the discs on newspaper and then cover with spray following the manufacturer's instructions. Allow the first side to dry before turning over and spraying the other side. Spray the two metal lamp rings with silver metallic paint to match the galvanized and jewellery wires, again working on newspaper in a well-ventilated area.

STEP 2
Wearing protective
goggles, cut six
70cm (28in) lengths
of 2mm galvanized
wire and bend each
in half to form the
template shape (A)
on page 132.

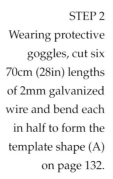

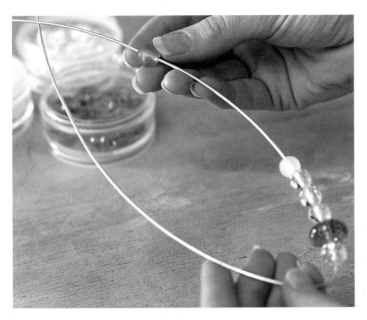

STEP 3
Thread the wire with an assortment of glass beads, in the same chosen pattern and colour scheme on both halves of the shaped wire.

STEP 4
Use round-nosed pliers to bend the ends of the wire into curls to match the template shape (B) on page 133.

STEP 5
Cross the wire over at the point shown on the template, arranging your design of beads so that some are above the cross-over point. Bind tightly with jewellery wire at this point to secure the shape. Repeat steps 3, 4 and 5 for the other five lengths of wire.

STEP 6
Use the jewellery wire to
bind the first shaped piece
to the large lamp ring. Bind
at the top of each curl, then
continue around the ring to
bind the next shaped piece
in position, and so on until
all six pieces are attached.

STEP 7
Use the jewellery wire to
bind the bottom point of each
shaped piece to the small
lamp ring, using the same
binding method as in step 6.
Stretch or compress the
shapes to fit exactly

STEP 8
Using jewellery wire, make loops to
achieve a scalloped effect around the
lower ring. Bind the initial piece of
jewellery wire to the bottom point
of one of the shapes. Thread with a
chosen pattern of beads and bind
to the bottom point of the adjacent
shape to form a loop about 4cm
(1½in) deep. Continue binding in this
way until all six loops are in position.

STEP 9

Using the 1.5mm galvanized wire, make six small pendant droppers to hang from the lower ring between each loop. For each dropper, take a 6cm (2½in) length of wire and bend a tiny loop in one end. Thread with your chosen pattern of beads, then make another small loop in the other end and attach to a small earring hook. Attach the dropper to the lower ring at the bottom point of the shape by hooking in place with the earring hook and squeezing closed with small jewellery pliers to secure.

STEP 10

Make six larger droppers to suspend from the cross-over points of the main wire shapes. Make each dropper following the method in step 9 but with a 10cm (4in) length of wire, and this time attach a small earring hook to both ends. Suspend a frosted glass shape from one earring hook and use the other earring hook to suspend the dropper from the cross-over point. Attach earring hooks to the final six frosted glass shapes and hang from a split ring positioned around the central point of the wire curls.

curtain-pole finials and holdbacks

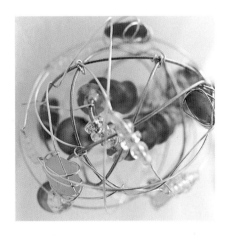

Tangled silver wire and glittering

beads in turquoise and white

combine to make up these unusual

finials and holdbacks.

These sculptural spheres are designed to sit decoratively on the ends of a ready-made silver curtain pole and matching holdbacks. The tangled wire ball is made from a frame of strong galvanized wire reinforced with silver jewellery wire. To introduce colour and light, the wires are threaded with a combination of beads and wrapped around frosted glass nuggets. The light, translucent style of these spheres works particularly well with simple white voile curtains that act to diffuse the light.

materials & equipment

2mm galvanized wire

pliers

protective goggles

assorted clear glass, frosted and blue beads in different sizes, some with large holes to thread on 2mm galvanized wire

metallic curtain pole (hollow to measure at least 8mm/⅜in diameter) and holdbacks to match

1mm silver-plated jewellery wire

small jewellery pliers

white and blue frosted glass nuggets

SAFETY NOTE

Wire can be sharp, so always wear goggles to protect your eyes.

STEP 1

Using pliers, and wearing protective goggles, cut a 25cm (10in) length of 2mm galvanized wire and bend it in half. Thread with large-holed glass beads in your chosen pattern on both halves of the bent wire, then bend the ends of the wire at a slight angle to form 'tails'. Push the tails into one end of the hollow metal curtain pole.

STEP 2

Cut another piece of galvanized wire about 1m (40in) long, tuck one end down into the hollow pole and then wind the wire around the central bead loop in a random fashion to form a loose cage. Tuck the remaining end into the pole as before to secure.

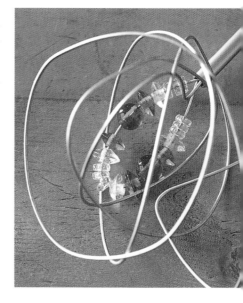

STEP 3

Cut a 1m (40in) length of jewellery wire and thread with a few small beads about 10cm (4in) from one end. Using small jewellery pliers, bend a small kink in the wire on either side of the beads to keep them in place.

STEP 4

Start weaving in the length of jewellery wire, using it to bind the cross-over points of the galvanized wire cage to hold it securely in place. Thread this wire with more beads, kinking it as before, and then continue to bind the cage. Finish the ends of the wire by winding tightly around the wire of the original cage. Use another piece of beaded wire if necessary to finish the binding so that the cage feels firm.

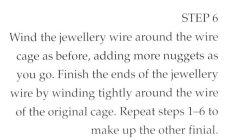

STEP 5

Cut a 1m (40in) length of jewellery wire and about 10cm (4in) from one end wind a length of the wire securely around a glass nugget in two or three directions, as shown.

STEP 6

Wind the jewellery wire around the wire cage as before, adding more nuggets as you go. Finish the ends of the jewellery wire by winding tightly around the wire of the original cage. Repeat steps 1–6 to make up the other finial.

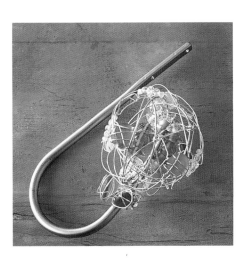

STEP 7

For the holdback, make a beaded and bound cage as for the finial but a little smaller. Using jewellery wire, bind the central tails to 7cm (2¾in) in from the end of the holdback, then bind a few glass nuggets around this to hide the bound wires.

the
bathroom

the bathroom

In many ways metal is an ideal material to be used throughout the bathroom for its easy-to-clean and waterproof qualities. However, bathrooms and restrooms that do incorporate metal are usually the expensive minimalist type, often seen in interior design magazines, or in commercial properties such as restaurants and offices. This look is derived from the recent fashion for metal surfaces and appliances in kitchens. In bathrooms, the metal is often combined with glass for a sleek, urban look. This style has been loosely translated in different ways by using aluminium in the form of framed shutters and galvanized steel to make a contemporary bath surround. At the other end of the spectrum, a rustic French country look can be achieved with a bathroom cupboard made of wire and, finally, for a bit of stylish fun, an often ignored metal material – foil sweet wrappers – has been used to cover a mirror frame.

Galvanized steel is the hardest material used in this book and the only one that requires specialist tools for cutting, so it is best to get it pre-cut by the supplier to the exact measurements you need. Once cut, holes can be made in it using standard tools. The bath panel shown here is made up from three pieces of galvanized steel pre-cut to fit the two sides and end of a bath. Often in a smaller bathroom the bath is boxed in between two walls and only one side panel is needed. This bath is fitted into a simple timber frame and the panels are screwed on to this. The design emphasizes the screw holes by making them an interesting industrial detail, adding decoration in the form of cogs from an old clock.

Shutters for bathroom windows are a functional and substantial alternative to blinds or curtains. Here, shutters were created with aluminium- and foil-covered frames and frosted glass panels to provide privacy. The panels are inexpensively

Use white and grey accessories to blend with the contemporary look of galvanized steel.

frosted using a glass-etching spray. The frames comprise a basic wooden structure clad in sheet aluminium and then decorated with a scalloped foil border. Their style is quite minimalist but with a decorative edge, as often seen in folk-art designs.

One of my favourite styles is French country, where an eclectic mix of old and new objects, some almost falling apart and some ornate with gilding and crystal, sit side by side. The small wirework cupboard was directly inspired by this style. Its beauty lies in the quirky, slightly wobbly design and the rawness of the materials used: chicken wire and pre-rusted iron wire. It is quite fiddly and time consuming to make but definitely worth the effort; the fragile look belies its strength and usefulness as a cupboard, although filled with pretty objects it is almost as decorative as a picture.

The balance of frame to mirror is quite important to the overall design. Here the frame is quite dominant and the mirror relatively small.

Foil sweet wrappers are often overlooked as a suitable material for metalcraft, but they do provide an exciting and (literally) fulfilling source of decoration. For the final bathroom project a circular MDF (medium-density fiberboard) mirror frame was covered with foil wrappers using the art of découpage. The wrappers were carefully picked for their colour, to work with the colour scheme of the bathroom, and their design; for added interest, plain wrappers were combined with others depicting small motifs. They are individually glued to the MDF in a random but nevertheless organized fashion. Sealing varnish is used to protect the mirror when finished. This idea translates well on to smaller frames or, if you are feeling ambitious, larger objects such as a chest of drawers or bedside table. The pattern of wrappers can be altered, using just two colours in a chequerboard effect, or a random multicolour design for a kitsch look.

steel bath-panel

Galvanized steel secured with cogs

from a clock mechanism makes an

interesting alternative to wood or

plastic for a bath panel.

G alvanized steel is the hardest form of metal used in this book. It can be cut to size and bent by the suppliers, in much the same way as a timber merchant would deal with wood. The best way to measure for bath panels is to install the bath into a timber frame and take measurements from the frame. The panels are screwed into place using chrome screws with the decorative addition of brass cogs and steel washers. The look is contemporary and urban and works well in a simple white bathroom scheme, surrounded by natural accessories.

STEP 1

Using a permanent marker pen, mark with a dot the drill-hole positions at the top, bottom and centre along both sides of the two corner pieces of metal. Place all the metal pieces on a safe surface, such as a few pieces of spare wood, before making the holes.

STEP 2

Place a centre punch on to the first marked position and hammer a few times to pierce the metal. Hammer a few more times to make the hole large enough for the screw to go through. Repeat for the rest of the holes. Mark dots at the top, bottom and middle of the short ends of both side panels, making sure these dots correspond with the holes on the two corner pieces, then mark dots at intervals of approximately 40cm (16in) along the top and bottom long edges of the side panels. Using a bradawl and hammer, pierce holes as before.

STEP 3

When the cogs are removed from the old clock, they will have a shaft through the centre. To remove this, simply place it over the hole in the end of a spanner (wrench) handle and hammer the shaft out.

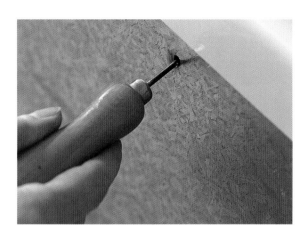

STEP 4

Offer up the panels to the sides of the bath, making sure they are correctly positioned underneath the lip of the bath. Using a bradawl, pierce a pilot hole through the metal into the wooden frame beneath.

STEP 5

Place a cog over each hole, then a washer, then screw both securely into the frame using a round-headed chrome screw.

STEP 6

When the side panels are in place, offer up the right-angled corner pieces, then screw them in place securely using cogs, washers and screws, as before.

framed shutters

Introduce diffused light into your

bathroom with a pair of decorative

aluminium-framed shutters.

The obvious solution to providing privacy at a bathroom window is to use frosted glass or opaque blinds. Here is another idea in the form of shutters that have come under the influence of modern technology and are made from wood, metal and etched glass. They provide privacy, security and decoration, and can be opened and closed. To make them, simple timber frames are clad with sheet aluminium. A scalloped tin border is placed on top of the frames to add decoration, and glass sprayed with etching spray is placed behind the frames.

materials & equipment

lengths of 18 x 70mm
(⅝ x 2¾in) and
12 x 45mm (½ x 1¾in)
timber, for frames

wood saw

wood adhesive

staple gun

panel pins and hammer

piece of 24 gauge
(0.5mm) sheet aluminium,
to clad frames

metal ruler

permanent marker pen

craft knife

tin snips

protective gloves

wet-and-dry paper and
sanding block

tracing paper and pencil

tin embossing sheets

scissors

bradawl

brass escutcheon pins

2 sheets of 4mm (⅛in)
glass, cut to fit recess

etching spray

length of quadrant, to fix
glass into recess

3 pairs of flush hinges

screwdriver

STEP 1

Using a wood saw, cut the wider timber into lengths to make two identical rectangular frames to fit your window space. Butt the pieces together at the corners as shown, then glue and staple to form the frame. Allow the adhesive to dry.

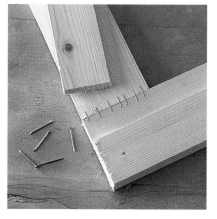

STEP 2

Cut the narrower timber into lengths to fit on the back of the frame, to form a recess into which the glass will be fitted later and to strengthen the join. Glue in place, then use panel pins to secure.

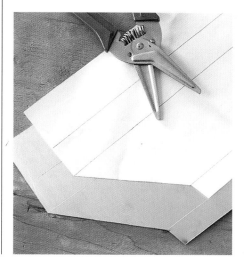

STEP 3

Enlarge the templates on pages 136–137 for the long and short sides of the rectangle, then extend where indicated to fit the size of your shutters. Following the templates, and wearing protective gloves, mark, cut and score the strips from the aluminium sheet (refer to the method on page 47, step 5). The template shows the mitre is curved for the shorter side, so when the pieces are in place there will not be a gap at the corner. Cut the curved line with tin snips. File the raw edges smooth with a sanding block to finish.

STEP 4

Enlarge and trace off the scallop template on page 138, extending where indicated, then use a pencil to redraw lightly over the template on to the tin embossing sheet. The metal is very soft, so a clear indentation will be made. Using scissors, cut out enough lengths to fit around the edges of the shutters.

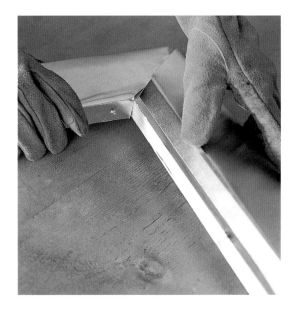

STEP 5

Wearing protective gloves, bend the aluminium strips along the score lines. Position the two shorter pieces around the frame at the top and bottom, and fix in place around the inner edge and at the back using panel pins. Then position the longer side pieces, pinning securely as before.

STEP 6

Place the scalloped strips on to the front of the shutter and bend the straight edge around the side of the frame. Trim and fold in the corners neatly, as shown. Use a bradawl to make a hole in each scallop shape, then hammer an escutcheon pin into each hole. Use panel pins to secure the straight edge to the shutter. Apply three thin coats of etching spray to one side of each piece of glass to achieve a frosted effect. Position the glass into the recess at the back of each shutter and then fix it securely in place using lengths of quadrant and large panel pins. Screw the flush hinges in place along the outside edges and fix the shutters into postion.

rusted wire cupboard

Reminiscent of antique French

wirework, this cupboard is made

from a combination of chicken

wire and rust-effect twisted wire.

T his pretty cupboard was inspired by a French antique version made from twisted wire which had been left to rust, adding to its charm. The body is made up from basic chicken wire, which is then reinforced with a twisted wire frame at the front and back. The excess wire on the frame and door is used to make decorative spirals at the front. Further decoration is added in the form of a flattened coil loop. Here, iron wire (left outside for a couple of days to rust) has been used both to aid strength and flexibility, and finally to bind everything in place.

materials & equipment

block of 25mm (1in)
MDF (medium-density
fiberboard), 29 x 22cm
(11½ x 8¾in)

piece of small-gauge
chicken wire,
60cm (24in) square

protective gloves

protective goggles

wire cutters

bent-nosed pliers

hammer

4 lengths of (0.5mm)
rusted iron wire, twisted
together to 6m (20ft)
approx (see page 130
for method)

2 lengths of (0.5mm)
rusted iron wire, twisted
together to 3m (10ft)
approx (see page 130
for method)

length of untwisted
(0.5mm) rusted iron wire,
3m (10ft) approx,
for binding

wooden spoon

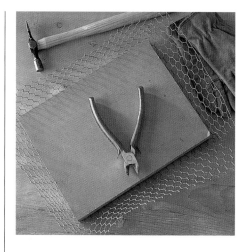

STEP 1

Lay the MDF block on the chicken wire. Wearing protective gloves and goggles, use wire cutters to cut the wire. Leave a 9cm (3½in) margin all round (cut as close to the honeycomb shape as possible to avoid leaving sharp ends). Cut out a square at each corner, leaving 1cm (¾in) overlapping the length of each side. Bend up the sides at right angles to the block of wood, using your hands and a hammer, to create a sharp right-angled bend.

STEP 2

Remove the block of wood and join the corners by bending over the extra 1cm (⅜in). Secure by weaving through, folding back and cutting off any excess wire.

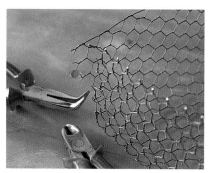

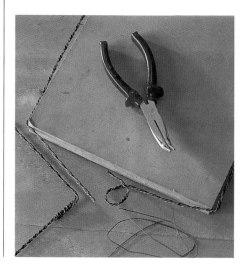

STEP 3

Cut a 110cm (44in) length of thicker twisted wire. Bend it around the block using bent-nosed pliers to make sharp right-angled corners. Remove from the block and join the ends with the binding wire. Trim the excess wire and lay aside. Cut another piece of thicker twisted wire 115cm (46in) long, bend it evenly around the block of wood and remove. With the two equal lengths at the top, make a loop with one length for hanging. Join it to the other length using binding wire and binding on either side of the loop.

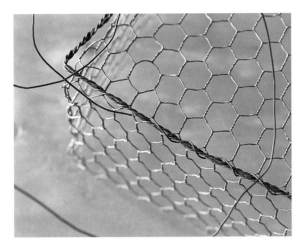

STEP 4

Place the back wire rectangle (with the hanging loop) on to the back of the chicken wire box and wire it into place tightly with binding wire.

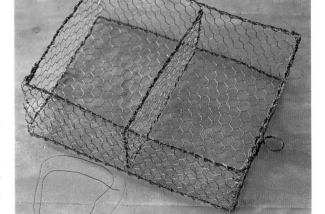

STEP 5

Attach the front rectangle in the same way; you will need to tuck under any protruding cut sections of the chicken wire. Make a shelf in the same manner, first measuring the internal space into which it is to be fitted. Wearing protective gloves, cut the shelf from the chicken wire. Frame with a length of thicker wire and fix it in place with binding wire.

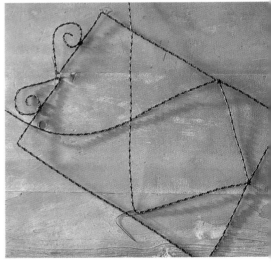

STEP 6

To make the door, take a piece of the thicker twisted wire 150cm (60in) long and bend it around the block, leaving equal ends at the top. Bend each one back on itself at the middle, remove from the block of wood and create the spirals as shown. Bind each one to the horizontal edge beneath it and bind the centre together temporarily.

STEP 7

Take another length of the thicker twisted wire and, with the binding wire, attach the centre of the length, which has been bent at a right angle, to the centre of the base of the door. Bring the two sides up and attach them in the same manner one-third of the way up the sides. Repeat two-thirds of the way up the sides as shown, and bring the two ends to meet between the loosely joined central horizontals beneath.

STEP 8
Undo the loose wire and tightly bind the four lengths together in a line. Turn the two ends into spirals as shown and bind together where they meet the original pair on either side and where they meet each other.

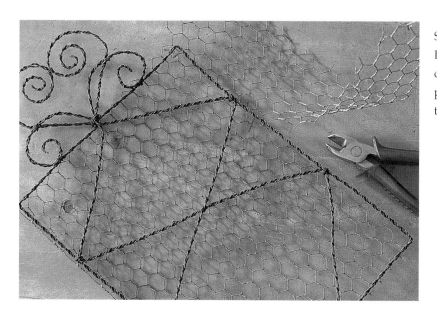

STEP 9
Lay the door on a piece of chicken wire and, wearing protective gloves, cut out the wire to fit.

STEP 10
Take the 3m (10ft) length of thinner twisted wire and wind it around the handle of a wooden spoon to make a long coil. Pull the wire off the handle and flatten the loops (see page 128 for method), then bind it on to the door edge, securing the chicken wire at the same time.

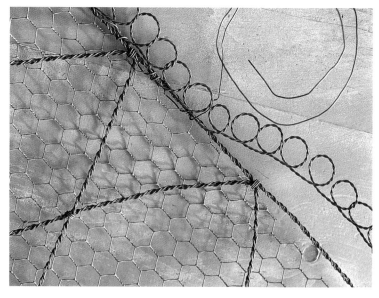

STEP 11

Make two simple hinges by binding the right side of the door to the box frame, in two evenly spaced places. Do not bind too tightly, to allow the door to be opened easily.

Decorative spirals are made from twisted rusted wire bound together for strength with single lengths of wire.

sweet-wrapper
mirror frame

Decorate a plain mirror with plain

and patterned sweet wrappers in

complementary colours to suit

your bathroom colour scheme.

F oil sweet wrappers are a wonderful source of material for brightly coloured, decorative découpage. Here they are used on a mirror, their colours carefully chosen to suit a scheme in the bathroom, comprising purple, mauve, turquoise, green and silver. Some wrappers are plain and some have pretty motifs which add interest to the overall look. The success of the design relies on the wrappers being positioned in a 'contrived randomness', where no two similar colours sit exactly next to each other, and there is a balance of colour over the whole frame. When complete, the frame is varnished for extra protection.

materials & equipment

circular frame of MDF (medium-density fiberboard), cut to preferred size (frame shown measures 55cm (22in) diameter for outer circle and 25cm (10in) for inner circle)

metal ruler

pencil

foil sweet wrappers

scissors

glue stick

shellac

paintbrush

mirror square, slightly wider than central hole of frame

4 mirror corner brackets and screws

screwdriver

2 strong D-shaped rings and screws

heavy-duty picture wire

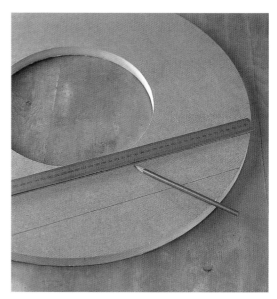

STEP 1

Using a pencil and metal ruler, mark out 6cm (2½in) divisions down the frame of the mirror. This gives you a guide for placing the sweet wrappers and is especially helpful if the wrappers you are using have a right-way-up design. Follow the pencil lines down the outer edge of the mirror frame and mark corresponding lines on to the back for horizontal hanging purposes.

STEP 2

After removing the chocolates (put them in the fridge and don't eat them all at once!) and carefully flattening the wrappers with your fingers, cut the wrappers into different-sized squares and rectangles to allow enough visual variation across the frame.

STEP 3

Rub the glue straight on to the base frame, covering one pencilled section at a time. Stick down the wrappers, gluing and overlapping them at the edges. The design looks balanced when similar styles and colours crop up at regular intervals.

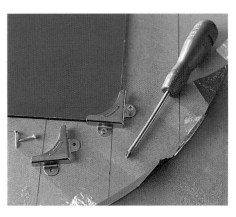

STEP 4

Continue gluing all the wrappers along the pencilled sections and then carry on down both the inside and outside edges of the frame. Loose corners can be glued to the back of the frame.

STEP 5

Apply two coats of shellac to protect the surface. Allow to dry between coats.

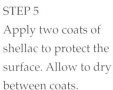

STEP 6

Turn the frame over. Using the pencil lines as your guide, position the mirror and screw the corners to the frame. Attach the two D-shaped rings along a pencil line about one-third of the way down from the top of the frame. Secure the picture wire to the two rings.

outdoors

outdoors

Metal is a natural element to be used outdoors, mainly for its hardwearing and weatherproof qualities. The obvious corrosive process with metal is its rusting, but none of the materials used for the outdoor projects here is susceptible to rust. All these items are suitable for the garden, or even the beach if you are lucky enough to have a garden overlooking one.

Even in climates that are not always fortunate with the weather, people are passionate about eating out of doors at any given opportunity. A summer's day can still be extremely hot in such areas, bringing with it the insects that are keen to devour unprotected food. One of the pieces has been designed to help with this problem, in the form of mesh and pewter food covers. Outdoor lighting is always important, and here candles really come into their own with a selection of wire-decorated jar holders. The other two projects are not so much functional as visual – and in one case also very audible. These are both made with sheet aluminium.

A good way of marking out your territory is with a monogram wreath hung on the front door; if you like the idea but would prefer a bit of privacy, the letter could always be changed to your door number. The wreath is made from a ring of galvanized twisted wire which is then decorated with cut leaf shapes, giving the impression of a classic laurel wreath. Your chosen letter (some work better than others on this type of wreath) is then glued in place using a special epoxy resin adhesive suitable for metal, so that no soldering is required. Wreaths are commonly placed on the front door during the festive season and this idea can easily be translated to accommodate a design for Christmas, Easter or other festivity.

Love them or hate them, wind chimes will always be around, particularly in ethnic craft shops, and come in a

Wire can be used to create an almost limitless variety of patterns.

variety of shapes, sizes and styles. If you are a fan of them, then you will know that it is quite difficult to find particularly decorative or attractive versions. Our version is customized with a large set of ornamental beaded butterflies that appear to fly around the top of the chimes. The butterflies are cut from sheet aluminium, which is then embossed and folded to give a three-dimensional appearance. Glass beads are added at the head and tail, and then each butterfly is attached to the wind chime via a length of twisted galvanized wire.

An embossed, beaded butterfly is used to decorate a set of windchimes.

Twisted, netted and spiralled wire make up the predominant metal feature in the glass candle jars. A selection of glass jars – ranging from old pharmacy jars to simple jam jars – were decorated on the outside with various designs in wire. These designs also incorporate handles, so that the jars can be hung in a tree or from a hook, or easily transported. Grouped together, they make an interesting centrepiece at an evening picnic. The most complicated design involves making a net from the wire with decorative beads linking it together. The same method can be used to cover and hold together stones in different sizes to make a paperweight or doorstop.

Finally, there is an idea for food covers to inspire you to replace any unsightly nylon versions that may be lurking in your cupboard! They have been designed with a bit of humour and feature pipe-cleaner bumble bees either sitting on their surface or buzzing around the edges, suspended from a length of wire. The covers' basic shapes are made using bowls around which you mould steel mesh. Many of the metal meshes available are manufactured for sculptural use and are very malleable, so this process is quite easy. The mesh shapes are then reinforced around the base and decorated with a scalloped pewter trim. Further embellishment is added in the form of wire flowers. These covers are so pretty that you won't be whipping them away and hiding them in the cupboard as soon as your guests arrive.

monogram wreath

Mark your home in style with a pretty monogrammed wreath made from silvery aluminium sheet and galvanized wire.

Monograms provide an elegant source of decoration in the home. They are used in many ways, particularly in soft furnishings and stationery. Here a monogram is introduced in the shape of a wreath, which can be placed outdoors – an unusual way of marking your residence or garden shed – or indoors to grace a mantelpiece or shelf. The aluminium sheet and galvanized wire that it is made from are both weather resistant in that they don't rust. An alphabet is provided on page 139 from which to choose your individual monogram.

An alphabet is provided on page 139 from which to choose your individual monogram.

materials & equipment

2 lengths of 1.5mm galvanized wire, twisted together to 95cm (38in) approx (see page 130 for method)

0.5mm galvanized wire

wire cutters

bent-nosed pliers

piece of 24 gauge (0.5mm) sheet aluminium, 60 x 30cm (24 x 12in)

masking tape

permanent marker pen

scissors

wire brush

tracing wheel

telephone directory

epoxy resin adhesive, suitable for metal

clothes pegs

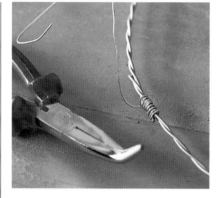

STEP 1

Bend the twisted wire into a circle with a diameter of approximately 29cm (11½in), overlapping 2cm (¾in) where the two ends meet. Bind together tightly to secure with the finer wire.

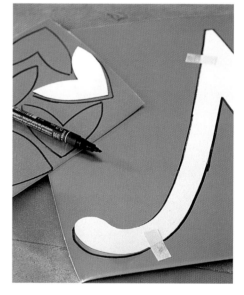

STEP 2

Make a paper template of a letter and leaf (see page 139). Choose your letter from the alphabet and enlarge it on a photocopier – the letter should be slightly larger than the wire circle in places so that it can be stuck to the circle. Attach the paper templates to the unprotected side of the sheet aluminium (one side is protected with blue film) with masking tape and draw carefully around the shapes with a permanent marker pen.

STEP 3

Remove the paper templates and cut out the shapes using scissors. It may help to change to smaller scissors when cutting around internal curves. Repeat to make as many leaves as you need.

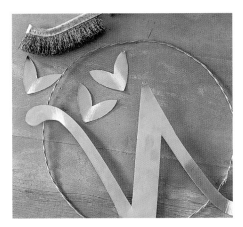

STEP 4

Using the wire brush and working on the back of the metal, brush the centre base of the leaves where they will adhere to the wire circle. Place the letter on to the circle in the desired position and, as with the leaves, abrade the areas where it contacts the wire.

STEP 5

Working on the back of the metal and resting on a telephone directory, push the tracing wheel up the centre of each leaf. Turn the leaves over (blue side) and make a central line between the two leaves to create a three-dimensional effect.

STEP 6

Mix the adhesive according to the manufacturer's instructions (you can use a small piece of metal as a palette and another as a spatula). Put a small quantity on the letter (shiny side) where it has been wire-brushed and immediately secure it in place with a clothes peg until the adhesive sets.

STEP 7

Stick the leaves in place in the same manner, adjusting the position of each one and securing with a clothes peg until the adhesive is firmly set.

STEP 8

Allow the adhesive to dry for the specified time before turning over the wreath. Pull off the protective blue plastic film.

butterfly wind-chimes

Transform ordinary wind chimes

with light-catching aluminium

and bead butterflies suspended

from twisted wire stems.

S tone and water features are commonly used in the garden, but bright metal – particularly aluminium, with its rust-free qualities – is an ideal material for something a bit more sculptural. Here ready-made wind chimes are customized with ornamental butterflies cut from sheet aluminium, then given a three-dimensional effect with a dotted design on the wings and body using a tracing wheel and moulded shape. Beads maximize the light-catching effect, and the butterflies are suspended on twisted wire as though they are flying.

materials & equipment

piece of 36 gauge (0.2mm) sheet aluminium, 25 x 40cm (10 x 16in)

ballpoint pen

scissors

tracing wheel

small hole punch

wooden spoon

2 lengths of 1.2mm galvanized wire, twisted together to 2m (80in) approx (see page 130 for method)

wire cutters

protective goggles

assorted coloured beads (holes large enough to take twisted wire)

strong adhesive

bent-nosed pliers

medium-sized wind chimes

drill with small bit

STEP 1
Trace the butterfly template on page 142. Lay it on the aluminium sheet, hold it in place and draw around it with a ballpoint pen, making an impression on the metal. Repeat to make three more butterflies.

STEP 2
Cut out the butterflies carefully using scissors, cutting between the two wings right up to the body.

STEP 3
Use a tracing wheel to mark all around the outside of the body and the wings, marking horizontal lines across the body as shown.

STEP 4

Mark similar lines where the wings meet the body and a starred circle on each wing, as shown. Use a hole punch to make holes in each of these circles and on the head and base of the body.

SAFETY NOTE
Wire can be sharp, so always wear goggles to protect your eyes.

STEP 5

Bend the body section around the handle of a wooden spoon and flex the wings to create a more three-dimensional effect.

STEP 6

Cut a piece of twisted wire 1m (40in) long and thread it through the holes on the body and head, allowing approximately 6cm (2½in) to protrude at the head end. Thread a single bead on to the wire at this point and add three contrasting beads at the base of the butterfly. You may need to secure them with a dab of strong adhesive. Repeat with another 1m (40in) of twisted wire and a butterfly.

STEP 7

At the head end of the butterflies, open up the twisted wire using bent-nosed pliers and turn each side into a spiral to serve as antennae.

STEP 8

Using a drill, make four holes in a square formation in the wooden disc at the top of the wind chimes. Thread the wire with the butterfly attached through one hole and back up through the opposite hole. Attach the beads and another butterfly to this other end in the same way as in step 6. Open up the antennae as before. Repeat the process with the remaining length of twisted wire and pair of butterflies, threading it through the other two holes.

wire-handled lanterns

These charming outdoor lanterns

are made from old jars, wire and

beads, and look pretty whether

or not the candles are lit.

Made from the most basic of materials, these pretty lanterns will grace the garden or an outdoor dining table. They work equally well hung from a hook, nestled in a tree or free-standing on steps or a tabletop. Different effects can be achieved by choosing a variety of glass jars, from the antique pharmaceutical type to an everyday jam jar. A range of wires can be used, from glamorous silver-plated jewellery wire to rustic florist's wire, and the same goes for the beads. Each lantern contains a candle stabilized with fine sand.

materials & equipment

0.6mm silver-plated jewellery wire

wire cutters

protective goggles

old glass jars

ruler or tape measure

small pliers

high-gloss silver beads (with holes large enough to take two lengths of wire)

lengths of florist's wire

oval beads

SAFETY NOTE

Wire can be sharp, so always wear goggles to protect your eyes.

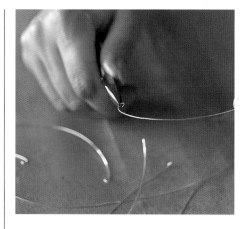

STEP 1

For the beaded-net design, use wire cutters to cut 16 lengths of jewellery wire to measure one-and-a-half times the height of your chosen jar. Using the small pliers, curve over one end of each of the lengths of wire.

STEP 2

Group the lengths of wire into eight pairs, then join each pair together with a single high gloss bead, as shown. To prevent the beads from sliding, bend each piece of wire outwards.

STEP 3

Take two beaded pairs and join them together by sliding a bead on to one wire from each pair, about 3cm (1¼in) down from the top beads. Keep a ruler handy to check this measurement. Again, bend the wire outwards to prevent the bead from sliding.

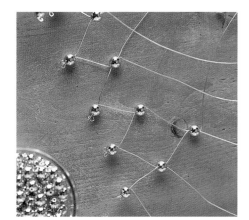

STEP 4

Repeat step 3 with more pieces of wire and more beads, until all the pieces of wire are linked together. Add a third row of beads using the same method.

STEP 5

Wrap your flexible net of beaded wire around the body of the jar and, taking up the loose ends along each vertical edge, join them with more beads using the method given in step 3, to form a seamless net enclosing the jar.

STEP 6

To attach the top of the wire net and provide a handle, cut a length of wire five times the height of the jar. Wrap the wire around the neck of the jar and secure one end by twisting it to itself to make a collar. Leave the other end dangling. With the pliers, take the little hooks at the top of the net and hook each one over the top of the wire collar. Take the dangling length of wire to the opposite side of the jar and at its half-way point thread it under the collar. Bring it back to its starting point by winding it back around the single-strand handle to strengthen. Twist a heart shape at the top of the handle. Tighten any slack in the wire collar by twisting it with the pliers. Cut off the surplus ends with wire cutters.

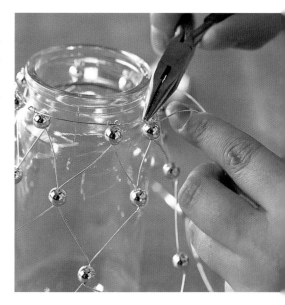

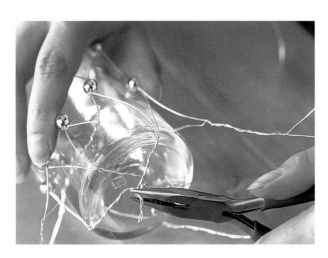

STEP 7

To finish the base of the design, place the loose ends of the wire into pairs as before and twist them from the point at the base of the jar. Then take each twisted section and join it underneath the jar to another twisted section on the opposite side of the jar. Continue until all the wires have been joined, then cut off any surplus wire using wire cutters.

STEP 8

For the wire-spiral design, take eight lengths of florist's wire and use small pliers to curl one end of each length around to make a spiral shape. Take the other end and twist a spiral in the opposite direction.

STEP 9

Using wire cutters, cut a piece of florist's wire approximately three times as long as the bead. Using the small pliers, curl one end of it, hook it on to a spiral and pinch it together. Thread the bead on to the wire, then cut off some surplus wire but leave just enough to make another hook to attach to another spiral. Link the spirals together in this way to make a collar for the jar. This jar had two collars, using four spirals per collar. Slide each collar on to the jar. Small circumference adjustments can be made to hold the collar in place by tightening or loosening the spirals. For larger or smaller jars, vary the number of spirals.

STEP 10

Twist a single length of florist's wire around the neck of the jar and secure. Cut off the surplus wire using wire cutters. Using the small pliers, hook a length of wire inside the collar on one side and another on the other side of the collar. Thread a bead on to each and twist the wire at the top to make a handle. Using the small pliers, spiral the tips to finish.

A paperweight or doorstop can be made using the same method as the beaded net jar. Replace the glass jar with stones and use a length of 1mm galvanized wire.

wire-mesh food covers

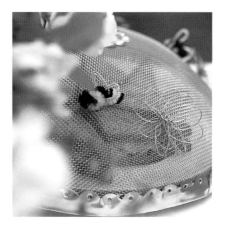

Keep marauding insects away

from your high tea on hot summer

days with these decorative metal

food covers.

These useful food covers are ideal for protecting food and can be used both indoors and out. They are made to fit over a dinner plate and a side plate, so the bowls that are used as a mould must correspond to these sizes. The main part of the cover is made from strong steel mesh, reinforced with an aluminium mesh band and a decorative pewter scalloped border. Skeletal wire flowers decorate the mesh expanse and charming bees, made from pipe cleaners, either sit on the mesh or 'fly' around it suspended from a length of wire.

materials & equipment

large and small bowls, for moulds

fabric tape measure

fine stainless steel wire mesh

permanent marker pen

protective gloves

scissors

pliers

aluminium or other pliable mesh

fine fuse wire

thin card

pewter sheet

revolving hole punch

high-tack, fast-drying adhesive, suitable for metal

1.5mm galvanized wire

black and yellow pipe cleaners

small beads

large bead (with hole large enough to take two lengths of wire), for handle

STEP 1

Turn the bowl to be used as a mould upside down and measure from one side of the rim, over the top, to the opposite side. Add 4cm (1½in) to this measurement and draw a circular template to this diameter. Use the template as a guide to cut out a circle from stainless steel wire mesh, wearing protective gloves. Start to form the mesh circle over the bowl, bending the edges under the rim of the bowl. Continue gently pressing and bending the mesh until it forms close contact with the bowl and the edges are bent over the rim neatly.

STEP 2

Pull the mesh off the bowl by unhooking the edges. Bend back the edges using pliers and trim to create a neat edge. Push the mesh back into shape if necessary. Cut a strip of aluminium mesh (or any very pliable mesh) 1.5cm (½in) wide and long enough to fit around the rim of the bowl. Join lengths if necessary by wiring the ends together. Lay the strip in position and stitch fuse wire through both layers of mesh all the way around to join.

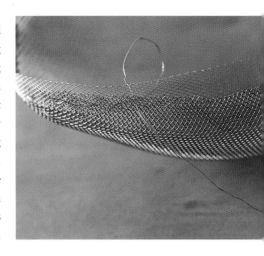

STEP 3

Use the scalloped edge shape on page 142 to make a template. Allow 2.5cm (1 in) to fold into the bowl. Lay this on the pewter sheet, draw around it using the permanent marker and cut out the required length of edging using scissors. Make a hole in each scallop using a revolving hole punch.

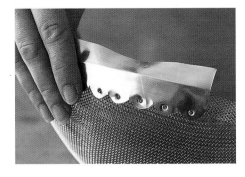

STEP 4

Mark the fold line along the pewter strip and carefully bend it over. Apply adhesive to the inside of the strip and stick it in position all around the rim of the bowl shape, smoothing out any folds in the pewter as you go.

STEP 5

Cut a piece of galvanized wire about 70cm (28in) long. Wrap it around your index and middle fingers, making about 12 loops. Remove the loops from your hand and thread a length of wire through the bottom of all the loops. Twist the ends of the wire together and pull the loops to form a flower shape. Wrap the wire around the centre of the flower a few times and leave a stem about 5cm (2in) long at the back.

STEP 7

Trace the scalloped circle template on page 142, then use to make a card template with a scalloped edge. Lay this on the pewter sheet, draw around it using the marker pen and cut out the scalloped top using scissors. Make a hole in each scallop shape using the revolving hole punch. Make a hole in the centre of the top and glue it in position. Push one end of a piece of wire through the hole in a large bead and thread small beads on to this. When the loop is the required size, push the other end of the wire through the large bead and twist to secure. Push this through the top of the food cover, open out the ends of the wire and glue in place. Thread, loop and secure the flower and bee stems through the mesh.

STEP 6

Cut a piece of black pipe cleaner to make the bee's body. Cut a piece of galvanized wire about 25cm (10in) long and make an antenna shape at one end. Wrap the wire around the bee's body and start to form a wing shape. Thread the beads on to the wire. When the wing is the required size, bend the wire under the bee's body and back up to form the second wing. Again thread beads on to it and bend the wire to form the second antenna, trimming the end if necessary. Wrap a short length of yellow pipe cleaner around the bee to make the stripes. Twist a piece of wire around the bee to form a stem.

technical information

materials and equipment

MATERIALS

The majority of the materials used in this book are readily available from hardware, craft, art and jewellery suppliers. Some of the thicker sheet metals and wires are only available from specialist suppliers. With the exception of the sheet metals and hardware companies, most suppliers operate a mail order service.

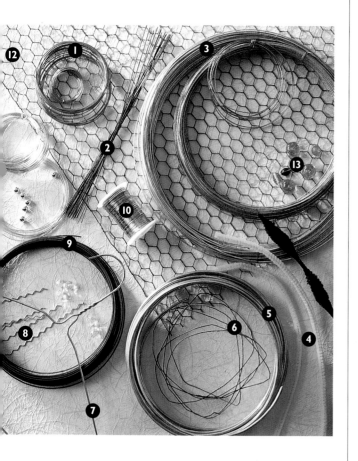

WIRE

Wire is made of solid metal which has the same cross section throughout and can range in thickness from a fine thread to a flexible rod. We most often think of it as having a circular cross section, but it can come in the form of a square or half-round, for example. In simple terms, wire is made by drawing rods of metal through different-sized holes in a drawplate to create wires of different diameters.

Wire can be measured by its diameter in millimetres and/or by a gauge. Confusingly, there are quite a few different standards for wire gauges, varying from country to country. In this book, wire has been supplied in millimetres.

❶ SOFT COPPER WIRE
Pliable wire with an attractive and decorative pinkish tone. Available in a variety of gauges from hardware stores and craft suppliers.

❷ FLORIST'S WIRE
Dull grey aluminium wire which is very pliable and easy to work with. Available from florist suppliers in pre-cut lengths.

❸ GALVANIZED WIRE
Steel wire with a zinc coat to protect it from rusting, making it ideal for outdoor use. This wire is hard and springy, so care should be taken when using it. Available in a variety of gauges from hardware stores.

❹ PIPE CLEANERS
These fibre-coated strips of wire come in a large range of colours and shapes and add additional interest to wire projects. Available from craft suppliers and department stores.

5 ALUMINIUM WIRE
This matt silver wire is soft, malleable and easy to work with. Finer gauges are available from craft suppliers. The thicker variety used for the Christmas-light sphere on pages 58–61 is available by mail order from specialist wire suppliers (see Resources).

6 IRON WIRE
Uncoated wire, rusted for an aged effect. Available from specialist wire suppliers (see Resources).

7 COAT HANGERS
A cheap, readily available source of thick, hard wire.

8 MODELLING WIRE
Steel wire with a zigzag shape, manufactured for use in clay sculpting. Available from art suppliers.

9 GARDEN WIRE
Easy-to-manipulate wire, coated with plastic. Ideal for outdoors as well as the kitchen and bathroom, due to its waterproof qualities. Available in a variety of shades and gauges from hardware and gardening stores.

10 FUSE WIRE AND FINE BINDING WIRE
Ideal for binding thicker wire pieces together. Available in a variety of finishes including tinned copper, copper and brass from hardware stores and craft suppliers.

11 SILVER-PLATED JEWELLERY WIRE
Fine, malleable wire with a bright silver finish. Available in a variety of gauges from jewellery and craft suppliers.

12 CHICKEN WIRE
Chicken wire is lightweight and malleable, although protective gloves should be worn when cutting it. Available in various gauges from hardware and gardening stores.

13 BEADS
A range of different beads have been used in the projects that involve wire, a perfect medium for threading. When choosing beads, attention should be paid to their hole sizes, making sure that they are compatible with the diameter of the wire used.

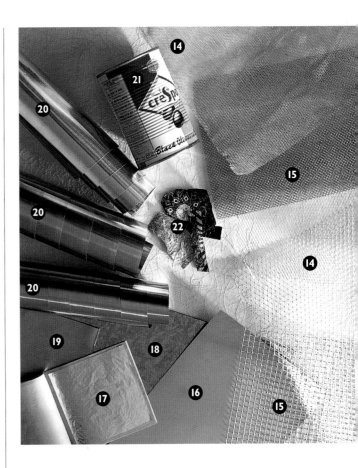

SHEET METAL AND MESH
Sheet metal is produced by passing metal through rollers to produce the desired thickness. As with wire, this thickness is measured in millimetres and/or by a gauge. Sheet meshes come in two forms: the fine, expandable variety, usually made from aluminium, and the harder, solid sort made from steel. Different types within a range are usually defined by the hole sizes, often specified in millimetres or by gauge.

14 EXPANDABLE MESH
Made from aluminium, and extremely soft and pliable. The holes are usually in the shape of a diamond, with different widths depending on the fineness of the mesh. Available from craft and art suppliers.

15 HARD MESH
Often made from steel, and very solid and impossible to mould, these meshes are available in various grid patterns and are normally supplied for outdoor domestic purposes. Very fine varieties are possible to mould. Available from hardware stores.

16 ALUMINIUM SHEET
Flexible but hardwearing form of sheet metal with a soft, matt silver finish. Available in a variety of gauges, widths and lengths from some hardware stores and specialist metal suppliers.

17 SILVER LEAF
One of the finest forms of sheet metal available, second only to gold. It comes in single sheets, sandwiched for protection between layers of paper. Available in a range of finishes and gauges from art shops and craft suppliers.

18 GALVANIZED STEEL SHEET
Hard, inflexible material with a mottled silver finish, which needs to be cut with specialist tools or by the supplier. Available in a variety of gauges from specialist metal suppliers.

19 PEWTER SHEET
Dull grey, soft sheet metal that is easy to work with. Available from craft suppliers.

20 COPPER, BRASS AND ALUMINIUM FOILS
Usually 0.1–0.2mm thick, these very fine, shiny foils are easy to cut and ideal for embossing. Available in roll form from craft and specialist metal suppliers.

21 TIN CANS
Plain or decorated tin cans are a good source of cheap and decorative sheet metal. Raw tin is sharp, so protective gloves should be worn when working with it.

22 FOIL SWEET WRAPPERS
Plain and decorated foil sweet wrappers are a good way of introducing colour to a design and are inexpensive and readily available.

EQUIPMENT

Most of the equipment used in this book can be found in a basic tool kit or around the home. The more specialist items such as tin snips, round- and bent-nosed pliers, a hole punch and a tracing wheel are available from hardware shops, department stores or craft and metal suppliers. It is important to wear protective gloves and goggles when working with the harder sheet metals, meshes and wires.

23 PLIERS
Useful for gripping and bending metal and wire.

24 ROUND-NOSED PLIERS
Ideal for bending small loops in wire and finer wirework.

25 BENT-NOSED PLIERS
Useful tool for bending and manipulating wire positioned in awkward places.

26 WIRE CUTTERS
Helpful for cutting wire and finishing ends neatly.

27 GILDER'S TIP
The best tool for picking up and positioning silver leaf without using your hands.

28 WIRE BRUSH
Used for brushing a metal surface to provide an abraded section for gluing purposes.

29 PANEL PINS
Small pins used to pin sections of the softer sheet metals to wood.

30 WET-AND-DRY PAPER
Fine sandpaper used for sanding metal in conjunction with a wooden block.

31 HAND FILE
Used for filing raw edges of metal.

32 WOODEN SPOON

Ideal tool to use when twisting wire.

33 HAMMER

Used for knocking in panel pins and hammering a centre punch when pattern making.

34 HIDE MALLET

Hammer made from densely rolled leather. Ideal for gentle hammering as it does not mark metal surfaces.

35 HAND DRILL

Useful tool to help with twisting finer wire.

36 HOLE PUNCH

Quick and effective way of making holes in metal.

37 CENTRE PUNCH

Useful tool for making decorative hole patterns in foil or harder metals, used in conjunction with a hammer.

38 STAPLE GUN

Ideal tool for securing chicken wire to wood.

39 PROTECTIVE GOGGLES

Wear these when carrying out work on metal and wire where small shards of the material may be produced or when springy wire is liable to backfire.

40 PROTECTIVE GLOVES

Use when handling raw cut edges of sheet metal, chicken wire and some of the harder meshes.

41 CRAFT KNIFE

Use a sharp craft knife for scoring and cutting some of the sheet metals.

42 TRACING WHEEL

Clever and quick tool for making embossed dotted lines on some of the finer sheet metals.

43 STEEL RULER

Useful for measuring and providing a hard edge for scoring lines in sheet metal.

44 BALLPOINT/MARKER PENS

A ballpoint pen without ink is the perfect tool for drawing embossed designs into fine foils. A permanent marker pen can be used for smudge-free marking.

45 PAIR OF COMPASSES

Useful for drawing out circles on to paper or directly on to metal.

46 MASKING TAPE

Ideal for applying directly to mesh and using as a guide for cutting out a drawn pattern.

47 SCISSORS

Can be used for cutting some of the finer sheet metals and meshes.

48 BENCH VICE

Useful tool for holding the harder sheet metals in place while filing and sanding.

49 TIN SHEARS

Heavy-duty scissors made especially for cutting hard metals.

50 TIN SNIPS

Less 'industrial' than tin shears, these scissors are designed for cutting metals. Good for cutting out smaller shapes and designs.

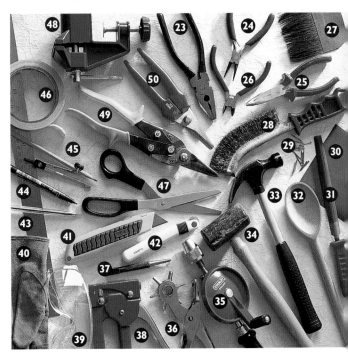

techniques

SAFETY

Metal is a hard material that should be treated with due respect and common sense when you are working with it. Care should be taken to wear protective clothing where appropriate.

It is advisable to wear protective leather gloves and hardy clothing when working with the thicker grade sheet metals such as tin and aluminium.

The same is advised for the tougher wires, particularly chicken wire and the stronger meshes. In some cases (specified in the project instructions), you should wear protective goggles, especially when cutting small lengths of wire or pieces of tin, as these can fly up into your face and cause injury.

Respect should be shown for the tools used to cut metal. These are obviously very powerful and should be kept in a safe place when not in use.

FINISHING RAW EDGES

Care should be taken with raw cut metal edges, particularly tin but also sheet aluminium. To ensure safety, it is best to finish metal by filing down any sharp edges. Always wear protective gloves and goggles when performing this task.

STEP 1 Hold the metal to be filed in place using a holding device such as a bench vice. Take a hand file, place it at right angles to the metal and then file using a forward-moving stroke, easing the pressure as the file is returned. Continue in the same manner until the complete edge has been filed.

STEP 2 Finish off the filed metal edge with wet-and-dry paper so that it is smooth to the touch. The wet-and-dry paper must be dampened first, then wrapped around a cork or wooden block before sanding along the metal edge.

EMBOSSING FOIL

Foil is a delightfully soft material to work with and can be decorated using a variety of techniques. These act to emboss the foil either from the front to achieve an indented effect, or from the back for a raised effect. The decoration can be done freehand or over a paper template.

USING A BALLPOINT PEN

One of the easiest and most effective ways to emboss your design is with an empty ballpoint pen. Simply draw freehand or follow the design on a paper template secured over the foil with masking tape. For the best results, carry out the embossing on top of a 'giving' surface such as a telephone directory.

USING A CENTRE PUNCH

A centre punch can be used to create an indented, pierced dot pattern on your chosen design that can also be reversed for a raised effect. First transfer your design on to paper and secure it in place on the foil with masking tape. Place the foil on top of a piece of wood to protect your work surface. Position the centre punch on the design and hammer once directly on top of the punch for each dot, working your way around the design to complete.

EMBOSSED EFFECTS

These freehand heart designs show the difference in the indented and raised effects.

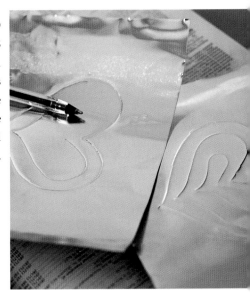

USING A TRACING WHEEL

A tracing wheel, which can be purchased in haberdashery departments, is an ideal tool for quickly and effectively decorating foil with a line or curve of tiny dots. Simply press down as if the wheel were a pencil and follow the design. For straight lines, use a metal ruler as a guide. Again, do this on a telephone directory for the best results.

TEMPLATES ON MESH

It is difficult to cut accurately around a paper template taped on the malleable meshes used in some of the designs. A good tip for achieving extra precision is to transfer your design to a 'sheet' of masking tape.

STEP 1 Take the piece of mesh and lay strips of masking tape side by side to form a sheet of tape, on to which you can transfer your design by pencil.

STEP 2 Cut out the shape following the pencil lines for a neat finish. Remove the masking tape.

MAKING A COILED EDGE

Wire coils flattened out to form a loop design make a useful decorative edging for a variety of projects. They work particularly well when used to finish off and disguise a bound edge, as in the celebration cake and rusted wire cupboard (see pages 26 and 88).

STEP 1 Wrap the wire around a rounded implement, such as the handle of a wooden spoon, a pencil or a broom handle. The diameter of the implement will determine how large the loops will end up. As you wrap, push the wire together several times. Continue winding, depending on how long you wish your loop edging to be.

STEP 2 Ease the wrapped wire off the implement and start to stretch it out. Flatten the loops with your thumb and forefinger as you go along. The loops can overlap each other slightly or sit apart, making individual loops.

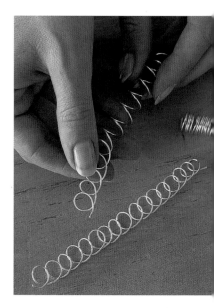

MAKING SPIRALS

Spirals are another popular form of decoration in wirework. They can be made loose and open or tightly bound together. They can also be made to follow two different directions from the same piece of wire, as in the wire-spiral jar (see page 114), or bound facing each other and back to back, as in the rusted wire cupboard (see page 88).

OPEN SPIRAL

First make a loop at the beginning of the wire using small pliers. Using your thumb and forefinger, carefully wind the wire around this loop, keeping the wire at a set distance from the loop and maintaining this distance as you continue to wind the wire to form the spiral.

CLOSED SPIRAL

Again make a loop at the beginning of the wire using small pliers. Using your thumb and forefinger, wind the wire tightly around the loop so that the wire touches the loop. Keep winding the wire in this way, using pressure to force the wire to form the tight coil.

SPRING SPIRAL

A spring spiral can be made by wrapping wire around a conical object such as an aperitif glass. Wire of a good strength, say 0.5mm, needs to be used for this method.

STEP 1 Leave a length of 3cm (1¼in) before holding the beginning of the wire firmly in place at the base of the cone with your thumb. Then start to wrap the wire around the cone, leaving a set distance between the turns of the wire.

STEP 2 Cut off the wire at the wider end of the cone where it wraps around to meet itself and remove it from the cone. Make a tight loop at the top of the spiral. For pretty Christmas decorations, thread with frosted and crystal beads to finish the spring spiral.

TWISTING WIRE

Twisted wire is often used in wirework designs and making it is a simple but essential technique to learn. It serves three main purposes: strengthening wire, while at the same time adding flexibility and introducing decoration. There are two methods, and both require the wire to be secured around a steadfast object such as a door handle or banister.

FOR TOUGHER WIRE

This method uses a wooden spoon. Cut the wire to three times your desired finished length. Bend the wire in half and loop the bent section around a door handle or bring it around a banister. Take a wooden spoon and twist the cut ends around the handle several times in an anti-clockwise direction. Hold the wooden spoon so that the wire is horizontal to the handle or banister and pull taut. Begin to wind the spoon in a clockwise direction to create the twist. Continue winding to achieve your required twist (the more you wind, the tighter the twist, and vice versa), holding the wire taut and horizontal to keep the twist even. Stop winding and then, holding the wire instead of the wooden spoon, let the tension release in the wire. Trim the ends with wire cutters.

FOR FINER WIRE

This method uses a hand drill. Cut the wire to double your desired finished length. Bend the wire in half and secure it around a door handle or banister, as with the tougher wire. Take the two cut ends, bind them with masking tape and secure them tightly in the chuck of a hand drill. Keeping the wire horizontal and taut, turn the drill to twist the wire. Release the wire from the chuck and trim the ends with wire cutters.

SAFETY NOTE

Twisting the tougher wires can be dangerous and in this case it is advisable to wear protective goggles and clothing. Because of the pressure used, letting go of the wires too early can cause them to backfire in an uncontrolled manner, accidentally causing injury.

METALLIC PAINTS

Metallic finishes are becoming very fashionable and as a result there is now an enormous variety of metallic paints, waxes and powders on the market. The larger paint companies have become aware of the demand and are now supplying metallic paints at affordable prices in larger pot sizes. Specialist paint and art shops have always been good sources of supply, but they, too, are extending their ranges to incorporate wonderful colours and iridescents, as well as the traditional shades of gold, silver and copper.

Spray-paints in traditional gold, silver and bronze are readily available from good DIY stores and art shops.

Unusual and striking colours such as purple, green, pink, and lustrous opalescents are among the range of new metallic paints now on the market.

templates

wire chandelier
enlarge by 40%

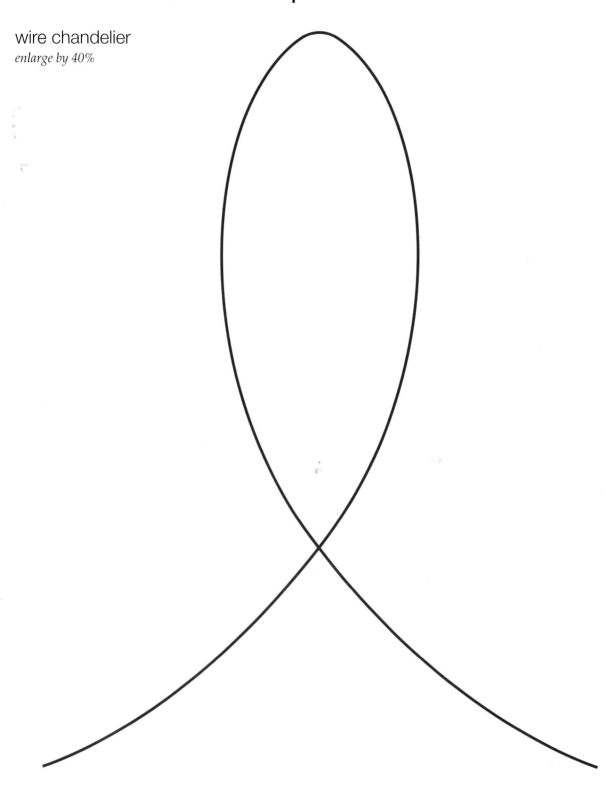

TEMPLATE A
WIRE SHAPE

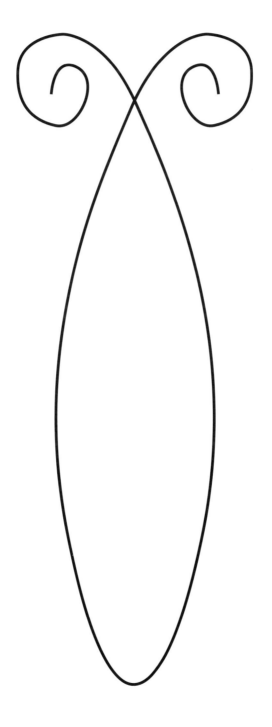

TEMPLATE B
CURLED WIRE

aluminium shelf

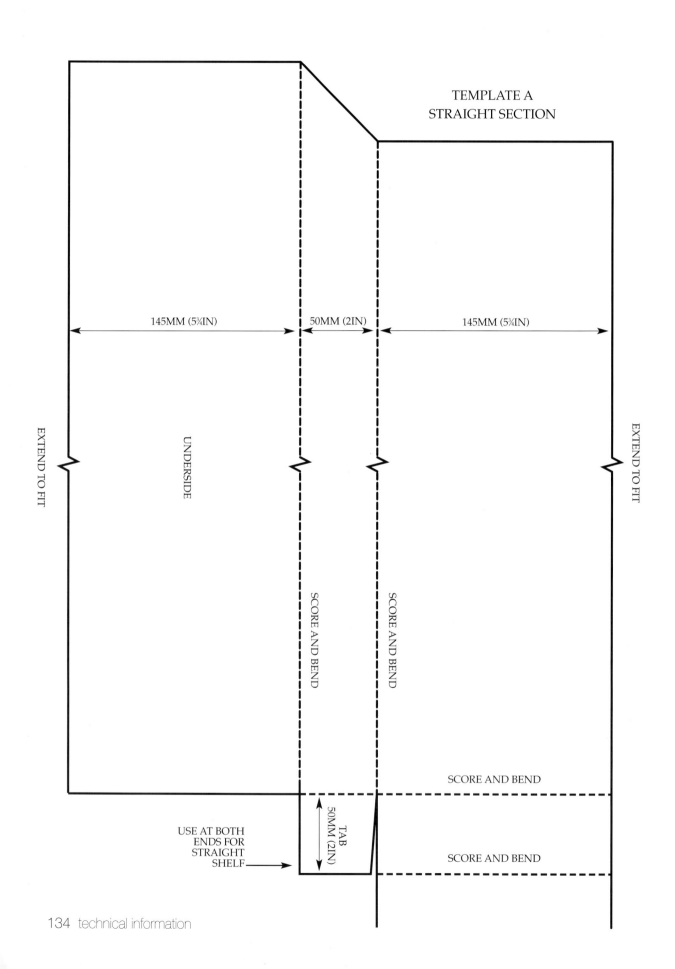

TEMPLATE A
STRAIGHT SECTION

145MM (5¾IN)　　50MM (2IN)　　145MM (5¾IN)

EXTEND TO FIT

UNDERSIDE

SCORE AND BEND

SCORE AND BEND

EXTEND TO FIT

SCORE AND BEND

USE AT BOTH
ENDS FOR
STRAIGHT
SHELF

TAB
50MM (2IN)

SCORE AND BEND

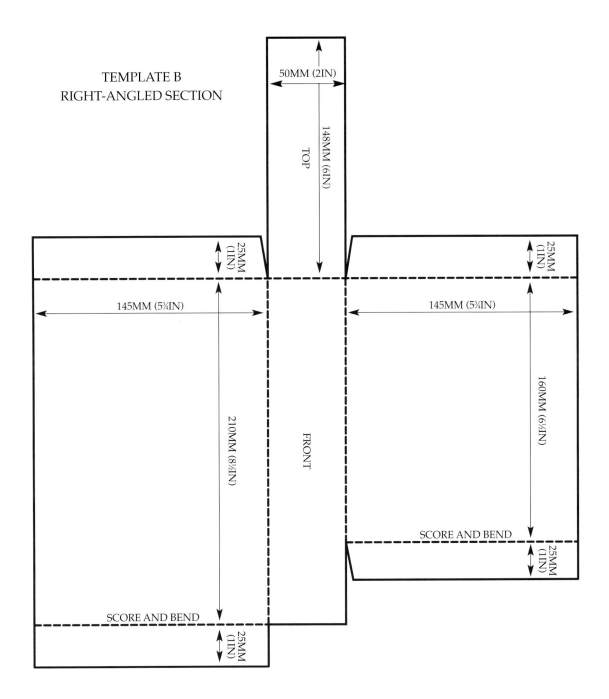

TEMPLATE B
RIGHT-ANGLED SECTION

50MM (2IN)

148MM (6IN)

TOP

25MM (1IN)

25MM (1IN)

145MM (5¾IN)

145MM (5¾IN)

160MM (6¼IN)

210MM (8¼IN)

FRONT

SCORE AND BEND

25MM (1IN)

SCORE AND BEND

25MM (1IN)

framed shutters

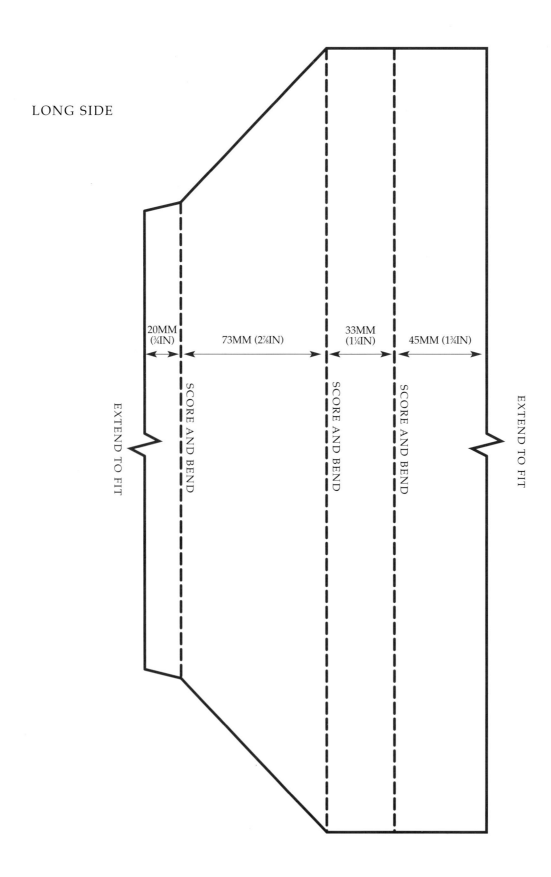

LONG SIDE

20MM (¾IN)

73MM (2⅞IN)

33MM (1¼IN)

45MM (1¾IN)

EXTEND TO FIT

SCORE AND BEND

SCORE AND BEND

SCORE AND BEND

EXTEND TO FIT

SHORT SIDE

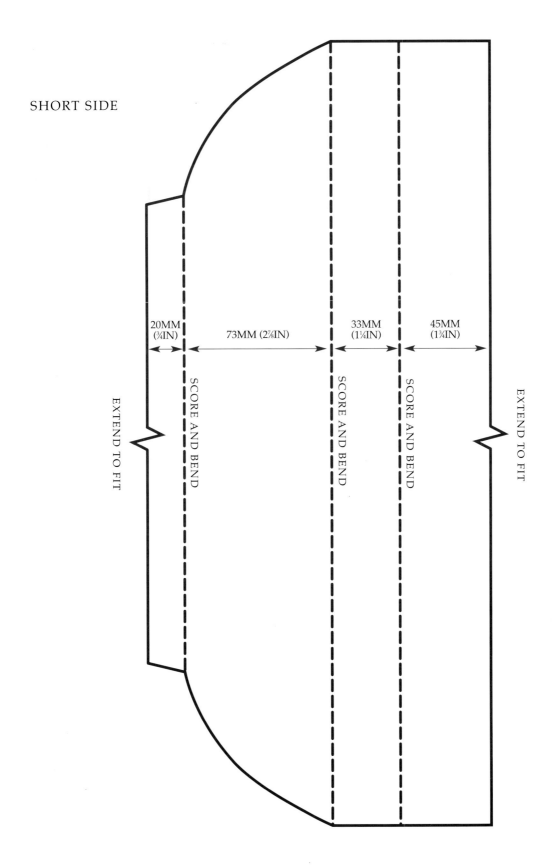

20MM (¾IN)

73MM (2⅞IN)

33MM (1¼IN)

45MM (1¾IN)

EXTEND TO FIT

SCORE AND BEND

SCORE AND BEND

SCORE AND BEND

EXTEND TO FIT

framed shutters

SCALLOP

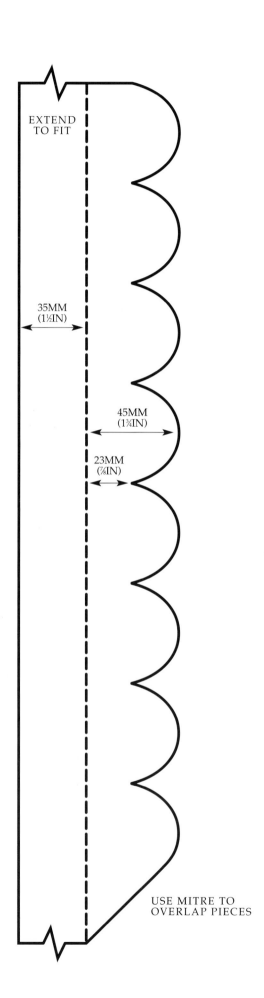

EXTEND
TO FIT

35MM
(1½IN)

45MM
(1¾IN)

23MM
(⅞IN)

USE MITRE TO
OVERLAP PIECES

monogram wreath

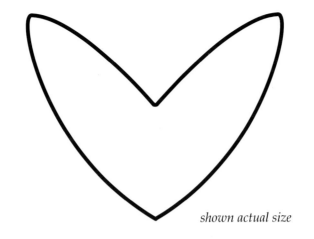

shown actual size

𝒜𝒜𝒜ℬℬ𝒞𝒞𝒟𝒟
ℰℱ𝒢ℋ𝐼𝒥𝒦𝒦𝒦
ℒℳℳ𝒩𝒩𝒩𝒪𝒫𝒫𝒫
𝒬𝒬𝒬ℛℛ𝒮𝒮𝒯𝒯𝒯
𝒱𝒱𝒰𝒲𝒲𝒳𝒳𝒴
𝒴𝒴𝒴𝒵ℰ

enlarge as required

decorative fire-surround
shown actual size

SUN

WIDE BAND

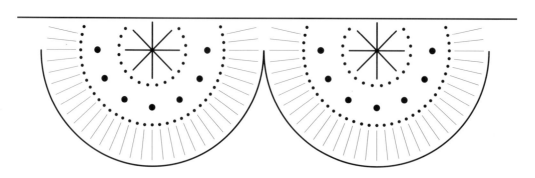

HEART

STAR

NARROW BAND

butterfly wind-chimes
shown actual size

wire-mesh food covers
shown actual size

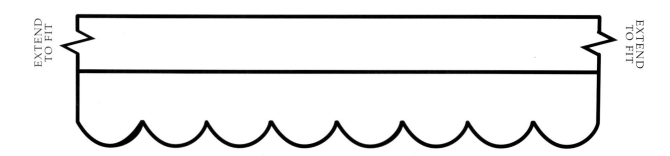

EXTEND TO FIT

EXTEND TO FIT

index

resources

UK

Fred Aldous
37 Lever Street
Manchester
M1 1LW
Tel: 0161 236 4224
Craft suppliers of foils, pewter sheet and some wires.
Mail order service available.

Cornelisson & Son
105 Great Russell Street
London WC1B 3RY
Tel: 020 7636 1045
Metal leaf, powders and associated gilder's tools.
Mail order service available.

George King
224 Tooting High Street
SW17 OSQ
Tel: 020 8672 8538
Sheet metal (including galvanized steel),
foils and wires.

The London Graphic Centre
16–18 Shelton Street
WC2H 9JL
Tel: 020 7759 4500
Art and craft suppliers of expandable
wire mesh and modelling wire.

Scientific Wire Company
18 Raven Road
London E18
Tel: 020 8505 0002
Specialist wires (including 3.25mm aluminium wire and
0.56mm iron wire for rusting). Mail order service available.

J. Smith and Son
42–56 Tottenham Court Road
London N1 4BZ
Tel: 020 7253 1277
Sheet metal, foils and wires.

Alec Tirantyl
27 Warren Street
London W1P 5DG
Tel: 020 7636 8565
Foils and wires.

US

Home Depot, U.S.A., Inc.
2455 Paces Ferry Road
Atlanta, GA 30339-4024
Tel: (770) 433-8211
Website: www.homedepot.com
Home improvement store with more than 1000 locations in
the US, Canada and abroad. Check the Store Locator on their
Website for the nearest location.

American Metalcraft, Inc.
2047 George Street
Melrose Park, IL, 60160-1515
Orders: (800) 333-9133
Fax: (800) 333-6046
Customer Service: (708) 345-1177
Request a catalog by phone or e-mail
info@ammtlcrft.com.
Hobby products include: aluminum, copper, brass, bronze,
stainless steel, foil, copper tape, tubing, and more.

Paragona Art Products
1150 18th Street, Suite 200
Santa Monica, CA 90403
Tel: (310) 264-1980
Supplier of soft copper, brass, pewter and aluminum foil.

Art2Art
432 Culver Blvd.
Playa Del Rey, CA 90293
Tel: (877) 427-2383
Fax: (310) 827-8111
Website: www.art2art.com
Assorted craft supplies available including
metals and wind chimes.

acknowledgements

I would like to thank the contributors who made
the projects, without whom this book would not
have been possible: Marion Elliot (tin splashback and
decorative fire-surround); Emma Hardy (wire-mesh
food covers); Jayne Keeley (sweet-wrapper mirror
frame, verre églomisé table, and wire-handled lanterns
and paperweight); Alison Jenkins (aluminium tabletop,
aluminium shelves, woven chair-seat, wire chandelier,
curtain-pole finials and holdbacks, panelled wardrobe,
framed shutters and steel bath-panel); Deborah
Schneebeli Morrell (fairy-light sphere, rusted-wire
cupboard, monogram wreath and butterfly windchimes); Lesley Stanfield (celebration cake and
greetings cards, and Easter ornaments).

I would also like to thank photographers Lucinda
Symons and Brian Hatton, plus assistants Emma and
Holly, for all their hard work and creativity, and
my commissioning editor Lindsay Porter and art
director Ali Myer at David & Charles for all their help
along the way.

Finally, I would like to thank the following UK shops
for lending items for photography:
The Pier (Tel: 020 7814 5020)
Damask (Tel: 020 7731 3553)
C.P. Hart (Tel: 020 7902 1000)
Next Home (Tel: 0870 243 5435)